Contents

Part Four

Answers to Worksheets and Notes for Use

Contents

Contents

Part Three

,

Test Your Grammar Skills

Troubling Tenses – What's the Best Time? 1

a) Complete each sentence with one of these words or phrases:

every day	yesterday	today	tomorrow	at the moment

b) Write the tense next to each sentence.

1. Andie was raiding the fridge _____ when her mum walked in.

2. Kathleen will have arrived in Sweden by _____ morning.

3. We have dinner at the same time _____.

4. Tim had stolen the man's wallet _____ for a dare.

5. We're waiting to use the photocopier _____.

6. I will book a taxi to take us to the airport _____.

7. I have managed to do some ironing _____.

8. _____ I catch the number forty train into work.

9. The birds are playing on the bird feeder in the garden

    _____.

10. We've been organising the office Christmas party _____.

11. Melanie will be attending the premiere _____ night.

12. We had been swimming in the lake _____ before the rain began.

13. I watched the sun sink slowly over the River Tyne _____.

14. I do Pilates to the same music _____.

15. I'm going to finish my project _____.

Test Your Grammar Skills

Troubling Tenses – What's the Best Time? 2

a) *Complete each sentence with one of these words or phrases:*

every day	yesterday	today	tomorrow	at the moment

b) *Write the tense next to each sentence.*

1. The children get back from school at about four _____.
2. Leah will be singing in the choir _____ evening.
3. The gate had closed and we couldn't fly _____.
4. We're going to ask the manager to give us a refund _____.
5. I'm trying to find the ink for the printer _____.
6. I've cleaned all of the downstairs windows _____.
7. I don't know why you have to be late for class _____.
8. They're having an important meeting with their suppliers

   _____.

9. My partner and I have been sorting through old photos _____.
10. We'd been walking for hours before we finally located the campsite

    _____.

11. We will have had breakfast by the time you get here _____.
12. Bob was cutting the grass in the garden _____.
13. The market begins at 6am _____ and stays open all

    morning.
14. June won't go to keep fit _____, because her back is

    playing up.
15. I put your pencil case back in the drawer _____.

Test Your Grammar Skills

Using Past, Present, and Future Continuous 1

Put the content words in SVOPT order (see p.64), then write one sentence in each tense (+, -, or ? form):

1.   make   pizza   kitchen   Paul

+ *Past Cont.* _____

- *Present Cont.* _____

? *Future Cont.* _____

2.   film   cinema   aunt   watch

- *Past Cont.* _____

? *Present Cont.* _____

+ *Future Cont.* _____

3.   friend   Terri   phonebook   add

? *Past Cont.* _____

+ *Present Cont.* _____

- *Future Cont.* _____

4.   spend   beach   time   Harriet

+ *Past Cont.* _____

- *Present Cont.* _____

? *Future Cont.* _____

5.   morning   brother   drive   Leicester

- *Past Cont.* _____

? *Present Cont.* _____

+ *Future Cont.* _____

Extension: *add a conjunction and a second clause to each sentence, e.g.*
'Paul was making pizza in the kitchen, because he was hungry.'

Test Your Grammar Skills

Using Past, Present, and Future Continuous 2

*Put the content words in SVOPT order (see p.64), then write one sentence in each tense
(+, -, or ? form):*

      1.   Italian   community centre   learn   father

+ Past Cont.   _____

- Present Cont. _____

? Future Cont. _____

      2.   photos   afternoon   you   look at

- Past Cont.   _____

? Present Cont. _____

+ Future Cont. _____

      3.   order   Kerri   chairs   client

? Past Cont.   _____

+ Present Cont. _____

- Future Cont. _____

      4.   Annabel   cathedral   wait   colleague

+ Past Cont.   _____

- Present Cont. _____

? Future Cont. _____

      5.   coffee   milk   Tom   put

- Past Cont.   _____

? Present Cont. _____

+ Future Cont. _____

Extension: *add a conjunction and a second clause to each sentence, e.g.*
'Her father was learning Italian at the community centre, but he found it so difficult.'

Test Your Grammar Skills

Using Present Perfect Continuous – have/has been + ing

All the residents of The Pine Trees Nursing Home in Orlando Avenue have gathered in the lounge for their weekly residents' meeting. The duty manager asks them what they have been doing all morning.

A) Complete the gaps below using the following words:

drying	chatting	washing	visiting	putting	waiting	throwing
feeding	clearing	knitting	staring	watching	doing	sitting
watering	playing	writing	reading	having	trying on

1. Jack says, "I've been _____ the plants in my room."

2. Mabel says: "I've been _____ the dishes in the kitchen."

3. Dolly says: "I've been _____ a letter to my great grand-daughter."

4. Arif says: "I've been _____ a quiz programme on TV."

5. Austin says: "I've been _____ the breakfast table."

6. Dorothy says: "I've been _____ the Guardian crossword."

7. Barry says: "I've been _____ the budgies."

8. Les says: "I've been _____ out of the window."

9. Harjinder says: "I've been _____ some new clothes."

10. Patrick says: "I've been _____ to my friends."

11. Gracie says: "I've been _____ photos in my photo album."

12. Maria says: "I've been _____ a sweater for my great niece."

13. Thora says: "I've been _____ in my armchair having a little sleep."

14. Hermione says: "I've been _____ my hair."

15. Jemima says: "I've been _____ my sister-in-law in hospital."

16. Barney says: "I've been _____ an argument with my daughter."

17. Samson says: "I've been _____ to have a go on the computer."

18. Luka says: "I've been _____ an interesting book about Russia."

19. Jonathan says: "I've been _____ pool with one of the nurses."

20. Thomas says: "I've been _____ food at people I don't like."

B) Ask and answer questions about the residents. For example: "What has Jack been doing?"

Test Your Grammar Skills

Using Past, Present, and Future Perfect 1

Put the content words in SVOPT order (see p.64), then write one sentence in each tense (+, -, or ? form):

1. tell   holiday   Alison   manager

+ Past Perf. _____

- Present Perf. _____

? Future Perf. _____

2. golf club   go   son   morning

- Past Perf. _____

? Present Perf. _____

+ Future Perf. _____

3. vet   dog   take   Charlie

? Past Perf. _____

+ Present Perf. _____

- Future Perf. _____

4. hang   hall   we   painting

+ Past Perf. _____

- Present Perf. _____

? Future Perf. _____

5. weight   Simon   year   lose

- Past Perf. _____

? Present Perf. _____

+ Future Perf. _____

Extension: *add a conjunction and a second clause to each sentence, e.g.*
'Alison had already told her manager about her holiday, so she didn't mention it last night.'

Test Your Grammar Skills

Using Past, Present, and Future Perfect 2

Put the content words in SVOPT order (see p.64), then write one sentence in each tense
*(**+**, **-**, or **?** form):*

1. clean   disinfectant   Kevin   sink

+ *Past Perf.*   _____

- *Present Perf.*   _____

? *Future Perf.*   _____

2. living room   she   curtains   make

- *Past Perf.*   _____

? *Present Perf.*   _____

+ *Future Perf.*   _____

3. email   receive   hotel   they

? *Past Perf.*   _____

+ *Present Perf.*   _____

- *Future Perf.*   _____

4. waiter   tourists   directions   ask

+ *Past Perf.*   _____

- *Present Perf.*   _____

? *Future Perf.*   _____

5. afternoon   run   Sheila's boyfriend   ten miles

- *Past Perf.*   _____

? *Present Perf.*   _____

+ *Future Perf.*   _____

Extension: *add a conjunction and a second clause to each sentence, e.g.*
'Kevin had cleaned the sink with disinfectant, but it still smelled a bit funny.'

Test Your Grammar Skills

Sentence Blocks – Present Perfect Continuous

Complete the sentence blocks:

Starting sentence A: **Jean has been doing her homework for twenty minutes.**

wh- question: **How long** _____

short answer: _____

yes/no question: _____

short answer: _____

yes/no question to
get a negative answer: _____

short negative answer: _____

long negative answer: _____

Extension: *make more sentence blocks using:* **who**, **what**, **whose**

Starting sentence B: **Our book group has been meeting in this cafe since 2004.**

wh- question: **Where** _____

short answer: _____

yes/no question: _____

short answer: _____

yes/no question to
get a negative answer: _____

short negative answer: _____

long negative answer: _____

Extension: *make more sentence blocks using:* **how long**, **whose**, **which**, **what**

Test Your Grammar Skills

Sentence Blocks – Past Continuous

Complete the sentence blocks:

Starting sentence A: **I was waiting outside my house for an hour, because I had lost my key.**

wh- question: **Why** _____

short answer: _____

yes/no question: _____

short answer: _____

*yes/no question to
get a negative answer:*   _____

short negative answer: _____

long negative answer: _____

Extension: *make more sentence blocks using:* **what, who, where, how long**

Starting sentence B: **Melanie and Steve were tidying their kitchen cupboards all morning.**

wh- question: **When** _____

short answer: _____

yes/no question: _____

short answer: _____

*yes/no question to
get a negative answer:*   _____

short negative answer: _____

long negative answer: _____

Extension: *make more sentence blocks using:* **what (x2), who, whose, how long, which**

Test Your Grammar Skills

Sentence Blocks – Past Perfect

Complete the sentence blocks:

Starting sentence A: Harry had eaten the last ginger biscuit to make Jack angry.

wh- question: Who _____

short answer: _____

yes/no question: _____

short answer: _____

yes/no question to get a negative answer: _____

short negative answer: _____

long negative answer: _____

Extension: make more sentence blocks using: **what (x2), which, what kind, why**

Starting sentence B: The delivery van had arrived before Mike got back from work.

wh- question: When _____

short answer: _____

yes/no question: _____

short answer: _____

yes/no question to get a negative answer: _____

short negative answer: _____

long negative answer: _____

Extension: make more sentence blocks using: **what (x2), which, what kind**

Test Your Grammar Skills

Sentence Blocks – Past Perfect Continuous

Complete the sentence blocks:

Starting sentence A: **We'd been jogging for an hour and a half, as part of our training programme.**

wh- question: **Why** _____

short answer: _____

yes/no question: _____

short answer: _____

yes/no question to get a negative answer: _____

short negative answer: _____

long negative answer: _____

Extension: *make more sentence blocks using:* **what, who, how long**

Starting sentence B: **The senior team had been working on the project for months, before making their final breakthrough.**

wh- question: **Which** _____

short answer: _____

yes/no question: _____

short answer: _____

yes/no question to get a negative answer: _____

short negative answer: _____

long negative answer: _____

Extension: *make more sentence blocks using:* **who, what** *(x2),* **how long**

Test Your Grammar Skills

Sentence Blocks – Future Continuous

Complete the sentence blocks:

Starting sentence A: **Mum will be waiting for you in the corridor after school.**

wh- question: **When** _____

short answer: _____

yes/no question: _____

short answer: _____

*yes/no question to
get a negative answer:*   _____

short negative answer: _____

long negative answer: _____

Extension: *make more sentence blocks using:* **who** *(x2),* **where,** **what**

Starting sentence B: **During the meeting I'll be presenting a series of challenging
questions.**

wh- question: **What** _____

short answer: _____

yes/no question: _____

short answer: _____

*yes/no question to
get a negative answer:*   _____

short negative answer: _____

long negative answer: _____

Extension: *make more sentence blocks using:* **when, who, what** *(x2),*
what kind

Test Your Grammar Skills

Sentence Blocks – Future Perfect

Complete the sentence blocks:

Starting sentence A: **Thomas and Anna will have been married for ten years on Friday.**

wh- question: **How long** _____

short answer: _____

yes/no question: _____

short answer: _____

yes/no question to get a negative answer: _____

short negative answer: _____

long negative answer: _____

Extension: *make more sentence blocks using:* **who, when**

Starting sentence B: **By the time you get to the restaurant, I will have ordered my main course.**

wh- question: **What** _____

short answer: _____

yes/no question: _____

short answer: _____

yes/no question to get a negative answer: _____

short negative answer: _____

long negative answer: _____

Extension: *make more sentence blocks using:* **which, what, when, who**

Test Your Grammar Skills

Could've, Would've, Should've 1

*Complete each sentence with **could've**, **would've**, or **should've**:*

use:	to show:
could have (could've)	that an action in the past was possible, but did not happen
would have (would've)	that an intention in the past was not carried out due to an obstacle
should have (should've)	there was a good reason to do an action in the past, but it did not happen

1. I _____ got a taxi,   but I wanted to walk.
    _____   because the college was five miles away.
    _____   but I didn't have enough cash on me.

2. Lyn _____ bought the dress,   but she couldn't afford it.
    _____   but she didn't like it that much.
    _____   because it would have looked great.

3. I _____ eaten the last cake, but I wanted you to have it.
    _____   because now I'm really hungry.
    _____   because nobody else wanted it.

4. The farmer _____ accepted help, because his business was failing.
    _____   but his wife talked him out of it.
    _____   but he didn't return the forms in time.

5. I _____ applied for that job, because I had the right qualifications.
    _____   but I found a better one.
    _____   because it would have been perfect for me.

6. I _____ parked near the school, but I didn't think of it.
    _____   because then we wouldn't have had to walk.
    _____   because I have a permit.

7. They _____ chatted for longer, because they both had nothing else to do.
    _____   but Wendy had to get off to work.
    _____   because they had so much to catch up with.

8. I _____ given you a lift home, because it started raining after you left.
    _____   but I didn't want to.
    _____   but my car is at the mechanic's.

9. I _____ unpacked the dishwasher, but I know that you like to do it!
    _____   but the phone rang and I got talking.
    _____   because it was my turn.

10. She _____ gone to the party, because she was invited.
    _____   but she was already going somewhere else.
    _____   because her favourite DJ played a great set.

Test Your Grammar Skills

Could've, Would've, Should've 2

*Complete each sentence with **could've**, **would've**, or **should've***:

use:	to show:
could have (could've)	that an action in the past was possible, but did not happen
would have (would've)	that an intention in the past was not carried out due to an obstacle
should have (should've)	there was a good reason to do an action in the past, but it did not happen

1. We _____ rented a movie,   because there was nothing on TV.
   _____   but our internet connection crashed.
   _____   but I wasn't in the mood.

2. I _____ washed the car,   but my son desperately wanted to do it.
   _____   but the car wash was out of order.
   _____   since it was absolutely filthy.

3. He _____ finished his thesis,   because it was due in the following day.
   _____   because he had had plenty of time.
   _____   but he had to make a few calls.

4. The lift _____ been mended,   but nobody made it a priority.
   _____   but an important part was unavailable.
   _____   because all the tenants hated the stairs.

5. It _____ been a great holiday, because it was a fantastic resort.
   _____   if it hadn't rained every day.
   _____   but we all suffered from stomach bugs.

6. We _____ won the election,   but we didn't receive enough votes.
   _____   because we really had the best policies.
   _____   if we'd appealed more to the middle classes.

7. Mia _____ assisted her colleague, since the project had been her idea.
   _____   but she was on vacation in France.
   _____   because she had the right level of expertise.

8. The novel _____ had a better reception, but three out of five stars was not bad.
   _____   if there had been more publicity.
   _____   because the writing was wonderful.

9. My friend _____ upgraded his mobile, if he had been able to find his contract.
   _____   but he didn't want the hassle.
   _____   because it was an old-fashioned brick.

10. They _____ applied for a loan,   but they didn't want to fall into debt.
    _____   because their credit rating was pretty good.
    _____   because it would have been the best option.

Test Your Grammar Skills

5 Forms of the Verb – 20 Phrasal Verbs (Movement)

Check any phrasal verbs that you don't know, then...

1) Complete the table:

infinitive	s form	past tense	past participle	ing form
bumble around				
buzz off				
catch up with				
come over				
drive off				
drop off				
fall over				
get off				
hurry up				
keel over				
keep up with				
melt away				
pass by				
pop round				
queue up				
roll around				
sidle up				
topple over				
turn up				
walk off				

2) Choose a phrasal verb (infinitive) and a tense and write 3 sentences – positive, negative, and question:

a) Infinitive: _____ Tense: _____

+ _____

- _____

? _____

b) Infinitive: _____ Tense: _____

+ _____

- _____

? _____

Test Your Grammar Skills

5 Forms of the Verb – 20 Phrasal Verbs (Communication)

Check any phrasal verbs that you don't know, then...

1) *Complete the table:*

infinitive	s form	past tense	past participle	ing form
agree with				
answer back				
blurt out				
chime in with				
disagree with				
drone on				
fob off				
get across				
gloss over				
hang up				
joke around				
mouth off				
open up				
point out				
quieten down				
rabbit on				
report back to				
speak out				
tell off				
write down				

2) *Choose a phrasal verb (infinitive) and a tense and write 3 sentences – positive, negative, and question:*

a) Infinitive: _____ Tense: _____

+ _____

- _____

? _____

b) Infinitive: _____ Tense: _____

+ _____

- _____

? _____

Test Your Grammar Skills

Write Your Own Verbs Challenge

Write 20 regular or irregular verbs (or a mix of both), then write sentences – positive, negative, or question form – using the given tenses and pronouns below:

For example:

+   choose   / pr perf / she   She has chosen to study politics at university.

1. + _____ / fu simple / I   _____

2. - _____ / pa cont / you   _____

3. ? _____ / pr cont / he   _____

4. + _____ / pr perf cont / she _____

5. - _____ / pa simple / we   _____

6. ? _____ / fu perfect / they _____

7. + _____ / zero cond / I   _____

8. - _____ / 1st cond / you   _____

9. ? _____ / pr simple / he   _____

10. + _____ / pr cont / she   _____

11. - _____ / 3rd cond / we   _____

12. ? _____ / fu perf cont / they _____

13. + _____ / pa perfect / I   _____

14. - _____ / fu with 'going to' / you _____

15. ? _____ / pa perf cont / he _____

16. + _____ / pr perfect / she _____

17. - _____ / fu cont / we   _____

18. ? _____ / pa simple / they _____

19. + _____ / 2nd cond / I   _____

20. - _____ / pr perf cont / you _____

Test Your Grammar Skills

Essential English Tenses Revision – Quiz

*Choose **true** or **false** for each of the statements below:*

1. Past continuous is used to talk about recent actions in the past.   t / f

2. Future perfect continuous is used to compare two actions in the past.   t / f

3. Future continuous tense uses ing form.   t / f

4. A future perfect action occurs after another future action.   t / f

5. In present perfect continuous we need to use have or has + being.   t / f

6. We use present simple for regular time and future actions.   t / f

7. We need to use past continuous to make 3rd conditional sentences.   t / f

8. A future perfect sentence often includes the words 'by' or 'by the time'.   t / f

9. Past perfect continuous is used to provide background information.   t / f

10. We use past simple when the time is finished.   t / f

11. Present simple is used to make predictions in the future.   t / f

12. Past simple is used to talk about life experience, e.g. 'Did you ever...?' t / f

13. A past perfect action takes place before a past simple action.   t / f

14. Present continuous is used for now and future with a time phrase.   t / f

15. I can use future perfect continuous to talk about anniversaries.   t / f

16. Present continuous uses ing form, unless the time is future.   t / f

17. A future perfect continuous sentence needs three auxiliary verbs.   t / f

18. In present perfect we use have or has + been as auxiliary verbs.   t / f

19. We use present simple for actions which are happening at the moment.   t / f

20. We need will + infinitive to make future simple sentences.   t / f

Test Your Grammar Skills

Tenses Revision Game – Present Simple

TIME	FORM
regular time	infinitive
FORM	**AUXILIARY VERBS**
s form (he, she, it)	do / do not (don't)
AUXILIARY VERBS	**AUXILIARY VERBS**
does / does not (doesn't)	if main verb is BE, use am, are, is
QUESTIONS & NEGATIVES	**TYPICAL TIME**
use infinitive	adverbs of frequency
USE	**USE**
regular actions	facts
USE	**EXTRA INFO**
future – timetables	state verbs use this tense

Test Your Grammar Skills

Tenses Revision Game – Present Continuous

TIME	TIME
now	future (+ time)
FORM	**AUXILIARY VERBS**
ing form (present participle)	am (I'm) / am not (I'm not)
AUXILIARY VERBS	**AUXILIARY VERBS**
are ('re) / are not (aren't)	is ('s) / is not (isn't)
TYPICAL TIME	**USE**
at the moment	continuous actions
USE	**USE**
temporary situations	arrangements (future + time)
USE	**EXTRA INFO**
repetition with always	state verbs cannot use this tense

Test Your Grammar Skills

Tenses Revision Game – Past Simple

TIME	FORM
past (finished time)	past tense
FORM	**FORM**
if irregular, learn the form(s)	infinitive (for questions and negatives)
SUFFIX	**AUXILIARY VERBS**
-ed (regular verbs)	did / did not (didn't)
AUXILIARY VERBS	**TYPICAL TIME**
if main verb is BE, use was, were	yesterday / last...
TYPICAL TIME	**USE**
...ago	completed actions in the past
USE	**EXTRA INFO**
to tell stories / news	the most common tense in English

Test Your Grammar Skills

Tenses Revision Game – Present Perfect

TIME unfinished time	**TIME** from the past up to now
FORM past participle	**FORM** if irregular, learn the form(s)
SUFFIX -ed (regular verbs)	**AUXILIARY VERBS** have ('ve) / have not (haven't)
AUXILIARY VERBS has ('s) / has not (hasn't)	**TYPICAL TIME** today / this...
TYPICAL TIME for + number / since + time	**USE** recent actions
USE life experience	**USE** when the action is past, but the time is not finished

Test Your Grammar Skills

Tenses Revision Game – Future Simple

TIME a specific time in the future	**FORM** infinitive
AUXILIARY VERBS will ('ll) / will not (won't)	**AUXILIARY VERBS** shall in question forms (suggestions)
TYPICAL TIME tomorrow / next...	**TYPICAL TIME** soon / later
USE immediate future	**USE** spontaneous decisions
USE predictions (think / believe)	**USE** promises
USE voluntary actions	**USE** first conditional

Test Your Grammar Skills

Tense Conversion – Practise English Tenses 1

Read the present simple sentence, then change it into 17 other tenses (where possible):

General Time:

1. *Present Simple:*   Mike plays golf with his mates twice a week.

2. *Zero Conditional:*   _____

Present:

3. *Present Continuous:*   _____

4. *Present Perfect:*   _____

5. *Present Perfect Continuous:* _____

6. *Imperative Form:*   _____

Past:

7. *Past Simple:*   _____

8. *Past Continuous:*   _____

9. *Past Perfect:*   _____

10. *Past Perfect Continuous:* _____

11. *Third Conditional:*   _____

Future:

12. *Future Simple:*   _____

13. *Future Continuous:*   _____

14. *Future with 'going to':* _____

15. *First Conditional:*   _____

16. *Second Conditional:*   _____

17. *Future Perfect:*   _____

18. *Future Perfect Continuous:* _____

For each tense:

Extension 1:   Write the **negative form** of the sentence, then a **question form** (yes/no or wh-)

Extension 2:   Write the three sentences in **reported speech**

Extension 3:   Write the three sentences in the **passive voice**

Extension 4:   Write the three passive sentences in **reported speech**

where possible!

Test Your Grammar Skills

Tense Conversion – Practise English Tenses 2

Read the present simple sentence, then change it into 17 other tenses (where possible):

General Time:

1. *Present Simple:*   I walk in the garden every day.

2. *Zero Conditional:*   _____

Present:

3. *Present Continuous:*   _____

4. *Present Perfect:*   _____

5. *Present Perfect Continuous:* _____

6. *Imperative Form:*   _____

Past:

7. *Past Simple:*   _____

8. *Past Continuous:*   _____

9. *Past Perfect:*   _____

10. *Past Perfect Continuous:*   _____

11. *Third Conditional:*   _____

Future:

12. *Future Simple:*   _____

13. *Future Continuous:*   _____

14. *Future with 'going to':*   _____

15. *First Conditional:*   _____

16. *Second Conditional:*   _____

17. *Future Perfect:*   _____

18. *Future Perfect Continuous:* _____

For each tense:

Extension 1:   Write the **negative form** of the sentence, then a **question form** (yes/no or wh-)

Extension 2:   Write the three sentences in **reported speech**

Extension 3:   Write the three sentences in the **passive voice**

Extension 4:   Write the three passive sentences in **reported speech**

where possible!

Test Your Grammar Skills

State Verbs Practice 1

State verbs describe states of being, including:

- *actions that happen in your head, e.g. **believe**, **know**, **want***
- *likes and dislikes, e.g. **like**, **dislike**, **love**, **hate**, **prefer***
- *senses, e.g. **see**, **hear**, **smell**, **taste***

They do not usually have continuous forms. <u>*Underline*</u> *the correct option in each sentence:*

1. Paula absolutely **loathed / was loathing** her new colleague's aftershave.

2. I **keep / am keeping** fit by exercising regularly and eating healthily.

3. We know that the children **lie / are lying** about who broke the DVD player.

4. The film **lasts / is lasting** for about ninety minutes.

5. I **think / 've been thinking** about going to Hawaii next year.

6. Alice **saw / was seeing** a comet when she visited the observatory last week.

7. Since Eric lost weight, his clothes **don't fit / are not fitting** him any more.

8. We **have / 're having** a barbecue on Saturday night, if you want to come over.

9. John **seemed / was seeming** really angry. What **does he want / is he wanting**?

10. I **have / 'm having** four puppies for sale, if you want to buy one.

11. Paul **has promised / has been promising** to lend me his guitar for years.

12. The weekend **consists of / is consisting of** five seminars and two practical sessions where you can **put / be putting** into practice what you have learned.

13. We **weighed / were weighing** the elephants for four hours yesterday.

14. I don't think you **realise / are realising** how much Bonnie is in love with you.

15. The boys **were / were being** silly in the lab, when the head teacher walked in.

Test Your Grammar Skills

State Verbs Practice 2

State verbs describe states of being, including:

- *actions that happen in your head, e.g. **believe**, **know**, **want***
- *likes and dislikes, e.g. **like**, **dislike**, **love**, **hate**, **prefer***
- *senses, e.g. **see**, **hear**, **smell**, **taste***

They do not usually have continuous forms. <u>Underline</u> *the correct option in each sentence:*

1. Be quiet! I **can't hear / am not able to be hearing** what he's saying!

2. I **love / I'm loving** your new conservatory. How much **did it cost / was it costing**?

3. This year we **involve / are involving** the whole company in the charity appeal.

4. When we visited grandpa he **didn't recognise / wasn't recognising** us.

5. They **drove / were driving** too fast when the police pulled them over.

6. I **don't mind / am not minding** how long you stay for. Make yourself at home!

7. We **relied on / were relying on** you to take care of our home while we **were / were being** away.

8. "**Do you fancy / Are you fancying** a trip to the mountains next weekend?" "Why not? That **sounds / is sounding** fantastic!"

9. I **defrost / 'm defrosting** the freezer so that we can get more food in it.

10. "Sorry you didn't get the job." "It's OK. It **doesn't matter / isn't mattering**."

11. My neighbour **doesn't believe in / isn't believing in** climate change.

12. We **tasted / were tasting** the most delicious cheeses for about an hour.

13. **Do you own / Are you owning** your own property?

14. "This contract is unreadable!" "Yes, I **agree / am agreeing** with you."

15. Charles **had wished / had been wishing** that Isabella would **notice / be noticing** him all evening.

Test Your Grammar Skills

150 Words which are both Verbs and Nouns

act	film	order	start
address	finish	paint	state
aim	fish	place	step
answer	flood	plane	sting
attack	flow	plant	stop
balance	fold	play	struggle
bear	form	post	study
benefit	function	process	suit
blame	guess	promise	supply
block	guide	protest	support
blow	heat	question	surprise
broadcast	help	race	taste
brush	hold	rain	test
buy	hope	record	trade
care	humour	repair	train
cause	hurry	reply	transport
claim	increase	report	trick
comfort	influence	request	trust
contrast	insult	rescue	turn
control	interest	respect	twist
cook	joke	result	type
copy	judge	return	use
crack	jump	ring	value
crash	kick	risk	visit
curl	kiss	roll	
curve	knock	row	*My ideas:*
cut	land	rule	
cycle	laugh	sand	_____
design	lift	search	
dislike	light	shape	_____
display	limit	shelter	
doubt	link	shock	_____
drink	look	shop	
email	love	show	_____
end	march	sign	
escape	mark	signal	_____
estimate	match	silence	
exchange	mind	sketch	_____
excuse	name	smile	
experience	need	smoke	_____
face	notice	sound	
fight	object	stamp	_____

Test Your Grammar Skills

Question Forms – Present Perfect Continuous

*Rearrange the words in each sentence to make a question in **present perfect continuous** tense.*

Don't forget to put a capital letter at the start of each sentence and a question mark at the end:

1.   all piano Mary afternoon playing the been has

_____

2.   to for years they the have nearly been campsite twelve going same

_____

3.   his for and have their donations been asking friends Roger brother

_____

4.   past for your half an teacher been hour talking has the

_____

5.   and you dolphins have whales this morning reading about been

_____

6.   him since Peter's have Saturday been with parents staying

_____

7.   a you brother's making for birthday your been have party cake

_____

8.   today bothering the have you newspaper been reporters

_____

9.   talking been Jason about has me

_____

10.   running outside dog her been all little around has day

_____

Test Your Grammar Skills

Question Forms – Past Continuous

*Rearrange the words in each sentence to make a question in **past continuous** tense.*

Don't forget to put a capital letter at the start of each sentence and a question mark at the end:

1. you the as leaving arrived was train just

   _____

2. you phone when kitchen going the were rang the into

   _____

3. most night posts of were reading on the you Twitter funny

   _____

4. you Tim's of meal my to were thinking mother birthday inviting

   _____

5. in yesterday annoying buzzing the was an manner bee around

   _____

6. you up about were in-jokes always Kevin making

   _____

7. uncle the running was when your began earthquake bath a

   _____

8. when their salad to the refusing grandma children eat were arrived

   _____

9. heading when exploded for it the was straight earth meteorite

   _____

10. Lena's a to former son husband was meet marriage going his from

    _____

Test Your Grammar Skills

Question Forms – Past Perfect

*Rearrange the words in each sentence to make a question in **past perfect** tense.*

Don't forget to put a capital letter at the start of each sentence and a question mark at the end:

1.   before had the going lights off you to all switched bed

_____

2.   since Road lived Jeremy in had 1989 Cromer

_____

3.   the out play their going pupils to completed had work before

_____

4.   John you left the got already had time home by

_____

5.   drunk half your somebody you from drink returned the when bathroom had

_____

6.   the made by call time his boss had appeared Liam phone a

_____

7.   school while a a ever still you had career at chef considered as

_____

8.   to gone phoned last bed had your them parents you just night when

_____

9.   had that seen already you movie

_____

10.   already meat out you the the been you cancelled bought before had party found that had

_____

Test Your Grammar Skills

Question Forms – Past Perfect Continuous

*Rearrange the words in each sentence to make a question in **past perfect continuous** tense.*

Don't forget to put a capital letter at the start of each sentence and a question mark at the end:

1. before meeting been for you arrive the starting waiting me to had

   _____

2. been holiday it day your ended the had before raining

   _____

3. painting had the morning been garage Philip all

   _____

4. Monday four you had Monopoly for both every playing years been

   _____

5. minutes caught twenty suspect had when about been for running you him the

   _____

6. since promoted you had florist's working the when at you got been Easter

   _____

7. meaning had the to been you tell microwave broken about me

   _____

8. an to been flight had catch hoping earlier Jessica

   _____

9. tablet before on been you games went out your playing had you

   _____

10. holiday you the Tom of your up already yesterday discussing brought cancelling it before had possibility been

   _____

Test Your Grammar Skills

Question Forms – Future Continuous

*Rearrange the words in each sentence to make a question in **future continuous** tense.*

Don't forget to put a capital letter at the start of each sentence and a question mark at the end:

1. taxi will this a you getting home evening be

_____

2. afternoon the in at o'clock a reading will two library tomorrow be Sue book

_____

3. fair helping you craft be next me the will at week

_____

4. having me exam later will thinking I'm you while be my about

_____

5. 6pm meeting tomorrow travelling at be to the Richard will

_____

6. party your to Tuesday on friends be will bringing the you

_____

7. few a landing we in be will minutes

_____

8. dance the collecting group will does be their money Steven while

_____

9. the spending to will listening be this year more government voters time

_____

10. again be this opening all late shops will the Christmas

_____

Test Your Grammar Skills

Question Forms – Future Perfect

*Rearrange the words in each sentence to make a question in **future perfect** tense.*

Don't forget to put a capital letter at the start of each sentence and a question mark at the end:

1. to gone by have get time I the you bed back will

   _____

2. end his by project have of week will next Terry finished the

   _____

3. most will the end of have the Jamie season by goals scored the

   _____

4. time restaurant the you will the up closes have cashed by

   _____

5. film tidied Trudie her the will starts room have before

   _____

6. one engineer problem fixed the will by o'clock have computer the

   _____

7. more by bus have you for than time the twenty arrives will the minutes waited

   _____

8. by have the you hairstyle again got you a will I see new time

   _____

9. seats get sold by I through time to the have the will ticket out shop best the

   _____

10. our by snowman it see Grandpa gets the have will to time melted

    _____

Test Your Grammar Skills

More Question Tags Using Modal Verbs 'can', 'will', and 'must'

Add an appropriate question tag to the end of each question.

*For example: She'll be late, **won't she?***

1. Gabriella won't let me use her hairdryer, _____

2. He must send the application form to us by the fourth of June, _____

3. My phone can download any apps, _____

4. You can't come to the press conference tomorrow, _____

5. We won't be back in the office until about one o'clock, _____

6. Wendy mustn't know about the new curtains yet, _____

7. John's grandma can bring Janey and Ali, _____

8. The others will be here in a minute, _____

9. We'll find out the results on Tuesday, _____

10. We mustn't forget to get some petrol, _____

11. Lucy won't mind if I borrow her dress, _____

12. We can't go swimming if the pool's shut, _____

13. I mustn't disturb Luis because he's working, _____

14. We can't stay for long, _____

15. Marco can drive us to the beach later, _____

16. The course will be over in a week, _____

17. It must be two years since we last met up, _____

18. Those girls can sing really well, _____

19. You must ask the office staff if you want to use the phone, _____

20. If you don't understand you can always ask the teacher, _____

Test Your Grammar Skills

More Question Tags Using Modal Verbs 'could', 'would' and 'should'

Add an appropriate question tag to the end of each question.

For example: *We could go to the bank later,* **couldn't we?**

1. You should get a refund if the gig is cancelled, _____

2. The learners who finish first could do some extra reading practice, _____

3. You should never switch off a computer without first closing it down, _____

4. You'd be annoyed if I talked all the way through Coronation Street, _____

5. I couldn't take you out for dinner tomorrow night, _____

6. Oliver should get to work on time every day, _____

7. The program couldn't be installed on your PC, _____

8. Sorry I'm late. The car wouldn't start, _____

9. We couldn't book a room for two nights, _____

10. The bar staff should be allowed to keep their tips, _____

11. Sheila could relocate to our Munich office, _____

12. We'd have to inform the students if the course was cancelled, _____

13. Look in the oven. The lasagne should be about ready by now, _____

14. We couldn't afford a new car last year, _____

15. The children shouldn't use the internet without permission, _____

16. You couldn't give me a hand with the gardening, _____

17. Mandy shouldn't wear that much make-up, _____

18. The managers could afford to give us more money, _____

19. We should all meet up more often, _____

20. Christopher wouldn't want you to be upset, _____

Test Your Grammar Skills

Mixed Conditionals 1

The term **mixed conditional** *usually refers to a conditional sentence which has past time in one clause and present or future time in the other clause (see examples below).*

a) Cut up the cards, mix them up, then match the sentences; or show one half of a sentence and elicit different ways to complete it. b) Discuss the times used in each sentence:

If I had read *Great Expectations* last month,	I wouldn't have to do it now.
I could afford to go on holiday next week	if I had put aside a bit of money each month.
I wouldn't have fallen for that practical joke	if I wasn't so gullible.
If we had bought a dishwasher,	we wouldn't be standing here washing up.
If Emily hadn't missed the bus,	she would be sitting here right now.
If Roger were more respectable,	he could have become a local councillor.
If I'd told my boss what I really thought,	I would be looking for a new job.
If the painting was by a famous artist,	it would have sold by now.
I wouldn't be able to wash my hair	if the shampoo had run out, would I?
If Tom hadn't met Mary,	they would both still be single today.
If we'd given up on buying a house,	we wouldn't be going to two viewings later.
If Tilly weren't allergic to dogs,	she could've become a dog breeder.
If I hadn't fallen off my horse,	I would be playing polo next weekend.
If I felt more strongly about your problem,	I would've done more to help.
If everything was fine at home,	I wouldn't have tried to run away.
I would be national champion today	if I'd won the 4000 metres.
If I *had* got married to Katie,	we would be much happier than we are now.
If I was able to move to Australia,	I would have done so long ago.
If Mark came to lessons more often,	he would've known about the test yesterday.
If I could leave home half an hour earlier,	I wouldn't have been late three times so far.

Test Your Grammar Skills

Mixed Conditionals 2

*The term **mixed conditional** usually refers to a conditional sentence which has past time in one clause and present or future time in the other clause (see examples below).*

a) Cut up the cards, mix them up, then match the sentences; or show one half of a sentence and elicit different ways to complete it. b) Discuss the times used in each sentence:

If I were you,	I wouldn't have eaten that many biscuits.
I would have been able to meet you	if it wasn't my day off tomorrow.
If I'd won anything less than first prize,	I wouldn't be happy with that, really.
If I knew how to change a tyre,	I wouldn't have asked you to help.
Jenny would be chatting to her mother now	if she'd been able to install Skype.
If I hadn't been so selfish towards my family,	I probably wouldn't be so lonely now.
If I knew someone who worked at the venue,	I wouldn't have had to queue up for tickets.
If the honey had cost £2 a jar instead of £3,	it would be sold by now.
I wouldn't have missed my lunch yesterday	if the lesson was from two to half past three.
If the sale at Wilson's was ending tomorrow,	I wouldn't have had to rush there last night.
If he'd found out that Jim had been stealing,	Brian would be absolutely livid now!
If you were me,	would you have asked your boss for a raise?
If Tim had left an hour earlier,	he'd be home by now.
If Jeffrey listened more,	he would've heard what I just said.
If I had known that it was your birthday,	I wouldn't feel so embarrassed now.
If I was able to pay my bills,	I wouldn't have defaulted on my mortgage.
If Minnie had practised the piano yesterday,	she wouldn't have to do it now.
If the circus was coming to town tomorrow,	I would've arranged to take my nieces.
If Simon had shared his problem with you,	it would all be sorted out by now.
I would still be in the waiting room	if the dentist had been really busy.

Test Your Grammar Skills

School Variety Show – Who Did What?

Passive Voice – Future (with will) and Past Simple

(Please see p.124 for full instructions.)

1. SHOW > **DIRECT** > BEN (MR. BRAHMS)

2. SONGS > **COMPOSE AND SING** > ALISON WATTS (MEGAN WATTS)

3. SCRIPT > **WRITE** > GRAHAM (GOK)

4. COSTUMES > **MAKE** > BARBARA'S MOTHER (MRS. PARSONS + TEAM)

5. SET > **BUILD** > TOM AND BEN (MR. ARTHUR AND BIG DAN)

6. SKETCHES > **PERFORM** > THE PETERSON TWINS (CARLY AND BEN)

7. SOUND > **OPERATE** > MIKE B. (GORDON RIDSDALE)

8. STAGE > **SWEEP** > CARLY (BIG DAN)

9. PROGRAMMES > **PRINT** > SCHOOL SECRETARY (TOM'S DAD)

10. CHAIRS > **PUT OUT** > OWEN (SCHOOL SECRETARY)

11. VENUE > **BOOK** > MR. BRAHMS (LOUISE HUDD)

12. MAKE-UP > **DO** > SANDRA'S MOTHER AND MRS. WHELK (OLIVE)

13. EVENT > **FILM FOR DVD** > JOCELYN WHISPERS

    (SILVER SCREEN PRODUCTIONS)

14. COFFEES AND TEAS > **MAKE** > MRS. PARSONS + TEAM

    (MR. PARSONS + TEAM)

15. PIANO > **PLAY** > GOK (MIKE B.)

16. CURTAIN > **RAISE AND LOWER** > BIG DAN (LITTLE DAN)

17. DANCE SEQUENCES > **CHOREOGRAPH** > LOUISE HUDD (GOK)

18. SCENERY > **PAINT** > MR. ARTHUR AND BIG DAN

    (THE PETERSON TWINS)

19. SHOW > **SPONSOR** > GLOVER INSURANCE (GLOBAL TRAVEL)

20. PROPS > **PROVIDE** > CARLY'S UNCLE CLIVE (LOUISE'S DAD)

Test Your Grammar Skills

20 Common English Phrasal Verbs – Mixed Tenses 1

Complete the sentences below with one of these phrasal verbs in the most suitable form:

do up	fall over	put up	mix up
brighten up	check out	get over	come across
cheer up	fall behind	keep up with	nod off
tidy up	grow up	hold on	give away
break down	break up	pick on	chat up

1. Have you noticed how our car _____ at least once a month?

2. It's all over the school how Maggie has _____ with Tom.

3. Lowry's Crisps _____ more than a million free packets by the end of this promotion!

4. We _____ the new facilities at the leisure centre last night.

5. Tina _____ at school, so we decided to find her a home tutor.

6. Paul _____ his flat all morning, because his girlfriend is coming round.

7. I _____ my coat and was just about to leave, when I realised I didn't have my keys.

8. Do you think Dawn _____ that waiter at the club again tomorrow night?

9. Some of the older kids _____ little Stevie at the youth club again.

10. These begonias are really going to _____ our living room!

11. Anita _____ a lot since she started college.

12. The twins _____ Christmas decorations all morning.

13. Our factory won't be able to _____ the demand, if orders keep flooding in.

14. If we go to a late show at the cinema, I always _____ before it's finished.

15. The problem with your interview was that you _____ as too self-assured.

16. I'd been trying to _____ my best friend, but then her boyfriend texted her back and she felt better.

17. The bass player suggested the band could _____ the set list for their next gig.

18. Lisa believes she will never _____ losing her engagement ring.

19. When the lift stopped suddenly Samuel _____ tightly to his mother's hand.

20. Roger _____ due to the thick ice that covered the pavements.

Test Your Grammar Skills

20 Common English Phrasal Verbs – Mixed Tenses 2

Complete the sentences below with one of these phrasal verbs in the most suitable form:

hold up	zip up	tell off	slow down
make up	let down	swot up on	log out of
work out	turn up	look after	take over
throw away	pipe down	think about	slog away
set off	leave out	put up with	walk in on

1. Incredibly, every year people in the UK _____ around 15 million tonnes of food!

2. My mate _____ me _____, because he offered me a lift but didn't turn up.

3. I _____ for work by the time you've made your first cup of tea.

4. Jo has got an exam tomorrow, so she _____ Tudor history all afternoon.

5. We _____ in the gym for twenty minutes, when there was a power cut.

6. The Robinson family _____ stray dogs for ten years by the end of this year.

7. I had already _____ the boys for playing football in the hall, but then one of them broke a window.

8. Sheila _____ at her desk all Sunday afternoon, while you are at the fair.

9. I _____ what you said, and it's true – we do need a holiday.

10. If you're going to _____ lies about me, then at least try to be original!

11. The police officer _____ the traffic due to a problem with a high-sided vehicle.

12. I've got to _____ Facebook and do something more productive!

13. Have you ever _____ your parents when they were in the middle of a massive row?

14. You can _____ your cardigan, or leave it undone – it's up to you.

15. Julie Falmer _____ as head of the lower sixth form from next term.

16. Look – Philip's just _____! I wonder what he wants.

17. Can everybody _____, please? I can't hear myself think!

18. The van _____, when it suddenly hit the kerb and span out of control.

19. I don't know how you _____ me, mum, but I'm so glad that you do!

20. Horace _____ bread for the birds since his grandma died last autumn.

Test Your Grammar Skills

20 Common Phrasal Verbs with Put

*It's time to learn 20 phrasal verbs with **put**, one of the most common verbs in English! Find out the meaning of any that you don't know, then write a sentence **with two clauses** for each one using the given form. Note: sby = somebody, sth = something:*

Example:

put across *past simple* *It was hard to put my point across, but I did my best.*

1. put across   present simple   _____

2. put away   zero conditional _____

3. put by   present cont.   _____

4. put down   present perfect   _____

5. put sby down   pres. perf. cont. _____

6. put forward   imperative form   _____

7. put sby through sth passive voice _____

8. put in   past cont.   _____

9. put into   past perfect   _____

10. put off   past perf. cont. _____

11. put back   third conditional _____

12. put on   future simple   _____

13. put out   future cont.   _____

14. put sby out   future w/going to _____

15. put sth to sby first conditional _____

16. put together   second condit.   _____

17. put towards   future perfect   _____

18. put sby up   future perf. cont. _____

19. put behind   mixed conditional _____

20. put up with   past simple   _____

Test Your Grammar Skills

20 Common Phrasal Verbs with Come

It's time to learn 20 phrasal verbs with **come**, *one of the most common verbs in English! Find out the meaning of any that you don't know, then write a sentence* **with two clauses** *for each one using the given form. Note: sby = somebody, sth = something:*

Example:

| come about | past simple | *We asked Neddy how the damage had come about, and he blamed his younger brother.* |

1. come with   present simple   _____

2. come across   zero conditional   _____

3. come apart   present cont.   _____

4. come away with   present perfect _____

5. come into   pres. perf. cont.   _____

6. come back   imperative form   _____

7. come between past perfect   _____

8. come by   past cont.   _____

9. come round   second condit.   _____

10. come from   past perf. cont.   _____

11. come in   third conditional   _____

12. come off   future simple   _____

13. come out with future cont.   _____

14. come over   future w/going to _____

15. come down   first conditional   _____

16. come out of   third conditional   _____

17. come together future perfect   _____

18. come up with   past simple   _____

19. come up against mixed conditional _____

20. come about   past simple   _____

Test Your Grammar Skills

Verb + Gerund (ing Noun) or Infinitive?

*These verbs are followed by **a gerund** (ing noun):*

admit	deny	involve	recommend
advise	despise	justify	reject
allow	detest	keep (on)	report
anticipate	discuss	mention	resent
appreciate	dislike	mind	resist
avoid	enjoy	miss	risk
can't help	fancy	not mind	save
carry on	feel like	postpone	suggest
complete	finish	practise	tolerate
consider	give up	put off	understand
defend	imagine	recall	
delay	insist on	recollect	

*These verbs are followed by **to + infinitive**:*

afford	decide	long	swear
agree	demand	manage	tend
aim	deserve	need	threaten
appear	expect	offer	try
arrange	fail	plan	turn out
ask	happen	prepare	vow
attempt	help	pretend	wait
care	hesitate	proceed	want
choose	hope	promise	wish
claim	intend	refuse	would like
dare	learn	seem	

*These verbs can be followed by either **a gerund** or **to + infinitive**:*

begin	continue	like	regret*
bother	forget*	love	remember*
can't bear	go on*	mean*	start
can't stand	hate	prefer	stop*
cease	intend	propose	

*These verbs change their meaning depending on the form that follows them

Test Your Grammar Skills

Gerund (ing Noun) or Infinitive? 1

Underline either a gerund or infinitive in each sentence below. Find 3 verbs that can be followed be either gerund or infinitive:

1. After two weeks of discussion we have agreed to give / giving you the job.

2. You would do well to avoid to take / taking the motorway this morning.

3. There would be an outcry if we publicly discussed to privatise / privatising the National Health Service.

4. It was tough, but Polly finally admitted to steal / stealing the jewellery.

5. If Harold had disliked to eat / eating the apple crumble, I wouldn't have offered him any more.

6. My daughter sometimes asks me to help / helping her with her homework.

7. I think you will really enjoy to meet / meeting my parents on Friday!

8. It can't have been easy for Barry to give up to smoke / smoking.

9. I hate to sit / sitting next to somebody who is eating an apple noisily.

10. Fiona had hoped to go / going to university in the summer, but now her dream had disappeared.

11. Can you imagine to hire / hiring a car on Sunday and just driving to the coast?

12. Holly had been learning to read / reading Braille since the beginning of term.

13. Did you manage to buy / buying the cake decorations that I asked for?

14. If I were you, I wouldn't mind to lend / lending Marina a few books.

15. By the end of the holiday we couldn't afford to eat out / eating out again.

16. Will you have practised to play / playing this piece on the trumpet by the time we meet again next week?

17. Alicia likes to read / reading in bed for a while before she goes to sleep.

18. I much preferred to visit / visiting Manchester compared to Huddersfield.

19. Charlie has been pretending to be / being an urchin from the film *Oliver* all morning.

20. If you would like to dance / dancing, I would be happy to accompany you.

Test Your Grammar Skills

Gerund (ing Noun) or Infinitive? 2

Underline either a gerund or infinitive in each sentence below. Find 2 verbs that can be followed be either gerund or infinitive:

1. Please consider *to ask / asking* your dad to let me borrow his lawnmower.

2. When the snow began *to fall / falling*, Elena sighed and pressed her nose against the window.

3. We have decided *to sell / selling* our bungalow and move to the French Alps!

4. I think their new production of *Hamlet* really deserves *to do / doing* well.

5. Do you fancy *to try / trying* that new restaurant that's opened down by the lake?

6. We need *to collect / collecting* ten more tokens before we can get the free watch.

7. Oliver's grandma had offered *to take / taking* care of the dog while they were away.

8. "Have you been watching *The Voice*?" "No, I keep *to miss / missing* it."

9. Is George planning *to invite / inviting* his cousin Albert to the family barbecue?

10. If people had continued *to buy / buying* CDs, the music industry would be in a better state than it is now.

11. My brother tends *to go / going* fishing at the weekend.

12. Will you have finished *to mark / marking* your students' coursework before lunch?

13. Laurence didn't expect *to receive / receiving* a single card on Valentine's Day.

14. Michael desperately wanted *to change / changing* his car for a more reliable model.

15. Sally missed *to spend / spending* time with her dad, who was working abroad.

16. The meeting seemed *to be / being* over, so Jack slipped out of the room and back to his corner in the canteen.

17. We recommend *to wear / wearing* the virtual headset for no longer than forty minutes without a break.

18. John was standing by his car frantically trying *to find / finding* his keys.

19. Alison's parents have promised *to buy / buying* her a tablet for her twelfth birthday.

20. When Pauline met up with her accountant for lunch, he suggested *to take / taking* the rest of the day off.

Test Your Grammar Skills

Gerund Fun 1

Underline the most appropriate word in each sentence:

1. Roland can't help **annoying / bullying** his sisters. He doesn't mean to!

2. Ben had never tried **walking / skiing** until yesterday afternoon.

3. Jane put off **calling / speaking** her aunt until the weekend.

4. Please make sure you wash your hands before **preparing / buying** dinner.

5. Tell Laura she looks nice, if you don't want to risk **telling / upsetting** her.

6. I can understand you not **trying / wanting** to talk about your ex.

7. Eddie decided that **telling / knowing** the truth was not always the best course of action.

8. When I first started **working / coming** here it was on reception.

9. After **visiting / holidaying** in Switzerland last summer, Elaine decided to move there.

10. Because we booked the flight online, we avoided **using / paying** the higher price.

11. I enjoy **cycling / training**. I'm going to run the London Marathon next month.

12. When pressed by his social worker, Luke admitted to **using / stealing** the phone.

13. Would you mind **standing / going** so that this lady with a baby can sit down?

14. Joseph's company had long been suspected of **falsifying / adapting** its accounts.

15. Don't miss **going / walking** to the match; it'll be a great day out!

16. Do you remember **meeting / recognising** Zafreen's cousin last year?

17. Did you sleep in a **sleeping / camping** bag when you went camping last week?

18. I don't mind **talking / covering** for you if you want to take the rest of the afternoon off.

19. I know you're angry about Philippe, but he's really not worth **worrying / upsetting** about.

20. Sarah and I spent a couple of days **relaxing / reminiscing** about the good old days.

21. I'm not used to **getting / going** the bus because I've always had my own car.

22. Young people should be encouraged to give up **smoking / studying**.

23. Do you fancy a trip to the **sporting / bowling** alley tomorrow night?

24. This bit of river is ideal for **fishing / playing**.

25. At midnight, Marya whispered to Nikolay, "I can't imagine **living / sitting** without you."

26. Odette loves to win. She can't stand **winning / losing** at anything – not even Twister.

27. If you continue **putting / kicking** your football into my garden, I'm going to keep it!

28. I tried taking **sleeping / eating** tablets to cure my insomnia, but they didn't work.

29. The teacher told two girls off for **talking / speaking** in class.

30. We really appreciate your **taking / putting** an interest in this case, inspector.

Test Your Grammar Skills

Gerund Fun 2

Underline the most appropriate word in each sentence:

1. Oscar put on his CV that his hobbies include **collecting / spending** rare coins.

2. I don't think that Halle is capable of **finishing / baking** that trifle on her own, do you?

3. "Did you have any problems **finding / meeting** us?" "No, the directions were fine."

4. **Making / drinking** tea after it's gone cold isn't my favourite pastime.

5. The main problem here is teenagers **being / having** nowhere to go in the evenings.

6. My brother simply isn't capable of **taking / holding** the initiative on anything.

7. Please be honest with me; there's no point **beating / running** around the bush.

8. I'm afraid I'm too busy to sit and watch you **waiting / getting** your hair cut. See you later!

9. Excuse me; do you know where the **waiting / living** room is, please?

10. Hugh felt a bit embarrassed about **showing / seeing** his grandma without her teeth in.

11. Turn right at the **swimming / playing** pool and the theatre is on your left.

12. **Learning / trying** to play the tuba should be a highly rewarding experience!

13. Please will you all just stop **messing / walking** about?

14. If you want my advice, **driving / running** would be quicker than **going / walking**.

15. Barbara always complains about Christmas **shopping / buying**, but she enjoys it really.

16. Did you know that Bob was taken to court for **watching / having** TV without a licence?

17. Would you mind **being / getting** quiet, please? We're trying to watch the news.

18. After Barry has done the washing up, he enjoys **spending / making** time with his kids.

19. Sita has real problems **drawing / remembering** maths equations.

20. Have you told Mr. Lees about **damaging / replacing** his car yet, Alan?

21. Betsy and Alan are very keen on **attending / driving** car boot sales.

22. Simon Cowell is famous for **speaking / making** rude comments on *X Factor*.

23. We didn't mention the burglary because we were afraid of **getting / losing** our jobs.

24. If it's a straight choice between **flying / travelling** and **arranging / catching** a train, then I'd rather fly, whenever possible.

25. Catherine apologised for **upsetting / chatting** her mum at lunchtime.

26. Are you interested in **taking / going** to the theatre one night next week?

27. If you have any problems **listening / ordering** our new CD, please email us.

28. "Hi, what can I do for you?" "Hello, I'm **wanting / looking** to open a new account."

29. I don't like **Dancing / Singing** *Queen*. I prefer ABBA's later stuff.

30. Carol warned her dad against **selling / buying** an old PC, but he bought one anyway.

Test Your Grammar Skills

Make a Sentence with SVOPT – Subject Verb Object Place Time 1

SVOPT (Subject Verb Object Place Time) is a very common form of word order in English. Complete the gaps in the sentences with your own words:

SUBJECT	VERB	OBJECT	PLACE	TIME
1._____	plays	2._____	on a barge	every Friday.
I	3._____	the minibus	4._____	last night.
The two parties	will have been discussing	5._____	in the boardroom	6._____
7._____	was printing	8._____	at the cybercafé	all morning.
We	9._____	our friends	10._____	before you turned up.
Louis	will have sold	11._____	at auction	12._____
13._____	going to hand in	14._____	at college	tomorrow.
Jodie	15._____	the tortoise	16._____	more than two months ago.
She	'll be waiting	17._____	by the kiosk	18._____
19._____	has been mulling over	20._____	in her apartment	all day.

Test Your Grammar Skills

Make a Sentence with SVOPT – Subject Verb Object Place Time 2

SVOPT (Subject Verb Object Place Time) is a very common form of word order in English.
Complete the gaps in the sentences with your own words:

SUBJECT	VERB	OBJECT	PLACE	TIME
1._____	is going to order	2._____	at that Italian restaurant	later on.
I	3._____	ten different dresses	4._____	this week.
He	's been looking up	5._____	in his dictionary	6._____
7._____	had ruined	8._____	in the new refectory	before security turned up.
I	9._____	some supplies	10._____	tomorrow at about eleven.
The whole team	will have been training	11._____	at the gym	12._____
13._____	had been depositing	14._____	in a high interest account	for decades.
Keeley	15._____	for her missing retriever	16._____	for forty minutes.
They	will have warmed up	17._____	in the microwave	18._____
19._____	was having	20._____	in that trendy new salon	after work.

Test Your Grammar Skills

Order of Adjectives in English 2

The order of adjectives is wrong in each sentence. Write the order of adjectives correctly:

1. I was reading an newspaper interesting old article. _____

2. It's going to be a major TV new series. _____

3. Do you want a glass of apple yummy freshly-made juice? _____

4. His uncle had a blue and white splendid cotton handkerchief. _____

5. I bought a set of painted miniature Estonian portraits. _____

6. Hugh used to be such an young skinny unpleasant guy. _____

7. We had seen mountain rocky majestic peaks. _____

8. George slid down the curved Victorian red banister. _____

9. He hadn't been down that dirt long bumpy road for a while. _____

10. Mum has just thrown out that brown old ugly pair of slippers. _____

11. Dan hadn't met the Spanish slim 18-year-old waitress before. _____

12. We partied in an Mexican beach exclusive resort. _____

13. Frank will've won a teddy furry cuddly bear. _____

14. He's discovered an techno astonishing new producer. _____

15. I was trying on an work cotton extra-large shirt. _____

16. The festival featured an short comedy offbeat film. _____

17. They had a long-distance difficult relationship. _____

18. The family will enjoy a sleigh Christmas magical ride. _____

19. We'd like to create a large living roomy room. _____

20. The archaeologist revealed an ancient unusual Mayan ritual. _____

Test Your Grammar Skills

Conjunctions Conundrum 1

and	addition	or	alternative
but	contrast (+ / -)	whereas	comparison
because	reason	even though	opposition
so	result	rather than	preference

Complete each sentence with four different clauses:

1. I woke up late this morning
    a) and _____
    b) but _____
    c) because _____
    d) so _____

2. It wasn't raining
    a) or _____
    b) even though _____
    c) and _____
    d) but _____

3. Michael won the race
    a) and _____
    b) whereas _____
    c) because _____
    d) so _____

4. I've just been paid
    a) even though _____
    b) so _____
    c) whereas _____
    d) and _____

5. We take the bus to work
    a) or _____
    b) even though _____
    c) because _____
    d) but _____

6. They will meet us tonight
    a) rather than _____
    b) or _____
    c) even though _____
    d) so _____

7. I must find my mobile
    a) or _____
    b) rather than _____
    c) because _____
    d) even though _____

8. We were getting angry
    a) rather than _____
    b) but _____
    c) whereas _____
    d) so _____

Extension: write five more groups of sentences with the same first clauses but four different second clauses.

Test Your Grammar Skills

Conjunctions Conundrum 2

and	addition	or	alternative
but	contrast (+ / -)	whereas	comparison
because	reason	even though	opposition
so	result	rather than	preference

Complete each sentence with four different clauses:

1. The parcel arrived late
   a) even though _____
   b) whereas _____
   c) because _____
   d) so _____

2. We drove to the museum
   a) but _____
   b) and _____
   c) rather than _____
   d) even though _____

3. Can I borrow a mug
   a) or _____
   b) because _____
   c) so _____
   d) rather than _____

4. Please redo your homework
   a) or _____
   b) but _____
   c) even though _____
   d) because _____

5. It was definitely Matt's fault
   a) and _____
   b) or _____
   c) rather than _____
   d) whereas _____

6. I made a fresh cherry pie
   a) rather than _____
   b) but _____
   c) even though _____
   d) but _____

7. She's missed the deadline
   a) and _____
   b) so _____
   c) whereas _____
   d) because _____

8. He will've eaten enough
   a) so _____
   b) and _____
   c) or _____
   d) whereas _____

Extension: *write five more groups of sentences with the same first clauses but four different second clauses.*

Test Your Grammar Skills

Use of Articles in English – Practice 1

*We know which article to use because of the **type of noun** and the **context** – general or specific.*

Below is a summary of the rules for using articles in English:

	Type of Noun:	Example:	Context:	Use this Article:
1.	singular countable	book	general	a (before a consonant sound)
2.				an (before a vowel sound)
3.			specific	the
4.	plural	books	general	zero article
5.			specific	the
6.	uncountable – concrete	water	general	zero article
7.			specific	the
8.	uncountable – abstract	music	general	zero article
9.			specific	the
10.	proper	Barcelona	N/A	zero article

i) Underline the noun in each sentence. Say what kind of noun it is
ii) Write **a**, **an**, or **the** in each gap, or put **-** to mean zero article
iii) Write a number 1-10 to show which rule the sentence follows

Type of Noun: Rule:

a) Do you often listen to _____ music?   _____ _____

b) He said _____ new employees were wonderful.   _____ _____

c) It was _____ second time I had asked you.   _____ _____

d) Is _____ chewing gum allowed?   _____ _____

e) I watched _____ good film yesterday.   _____ _____

f) She lived in _____ Paris.   _____ _____

g) I downloaded _____ app last week.   _____ _____

h) He often bakes _____ cakes.   _____ _____

i) I would like _____ biggest potato.   _____ _____

j) He always drinks _____ Coca-Cola.   _____ _____

k) I was surprised by _____ progress we made.   _____ _____

l) He has bought _____ new car.   _____ _____

m) She thought that _____ rice was a bit undercooked.   _____ _____

n) I wonder why _____ children love to play.   _____ _____

o) I ate _____ egg yesterday.   _____ _____

p) He didn't have _____ patience to be a teacher.   _____ _____

q) I showed her _____ red socks that I had bought.   _____ _____

r) We have already spent _____ money you gave us.   _____ _____

s) I believe that _____ perseverance is important.   _____ _____

t) He has got _____ short brown hair.   _____ _____

Test Your Grammar Skills

Use of Articles in English – Practice 2

*We know which article to use because of the **type of noun** and the **context** – general or specific.*

Below is a summary of the rules for using articles in English:

	Type of Noun:	Example:	Context:	Use this Article:
1.	singular countable	*book*	general	a (before a consonant sound)
2.				an (before a vowel sound)
3.			specific	the
4.	plural	*books*	general	zero article
5.			specific	the
6.	uncountable – concrete	*water*	general	zero article
7.			specific	the
8.	uncountable – abstract	*music*	general	zero article
9.			specific	the
10.	proper	*Barcelona*	N/A	zero article

i) Underline the noun in each sentence. Say what kind of noun it is
ii) Write **a**, **an**, or **the** in each gap, or put **-** to mean zero article
iii) Write a number 1-10 to show which rule the sentence follows

Type of Noun: Rule:

a)   He needs to cut _____ grass.   _____ _____

b)   He looks similar to _____ Darren.   _____ _____

c)   She doesn't like _____ ice cream.   _____ _____

d)   I used _____ green pen.   _____ _____

e)   She is looking for _____ work.   _____ _____

f)   Would you like _____ orange?   _____ _____

g)   This is _____ second photo that he took.   _____ _____

h)   We appreciate _____ dedication that you have shown.   _____ _____

i)   I think _____ students should always work hard.   _____ _____

j)   We arrived on _____ Tuesday.   _____ _____

k)   We'll get _____ petrol later on.   _____ _____

l)   I didn't have _____ courage that I needed.   _____ _____

m)   Sometimes _____ life is hard.   _____ _____

n)   I put on _____ coat and went out.   _____ _____

o)   I don't usually get _____ colds.   _____ _____

p)   We suggested _____ idea to her.   _____ _____

q)   They preferred _____ leather furniture.   _____ _____

r)   Did you understand _____ assignments from yesterday?_____ _____

s)   She picked up _____ book and started to read it.   _____ _____

t)   Are _____ chips ready yet?   _____ _____

Test Your Grammar Skills

Use of Articles in English – 40 Question Quiz

Write **a**, **an**, or **the** in each gap, or put **-** to mean zero article

1. He was born in _____ August.
2. John sells _____ bikes every day.
3. Do you want _____ spaghetti today?
4. It was _____ hottest day ever!
5. He prefers _____ Adidas.
6. I put _____ unopened letters over there.
7. Is _____ clock slow, or is it me?
8. Would you like _____ apricot?
9. We were moved by _____ kindness that he showed.
10. I got _____ puppy yesterday.

11. We've booked _____ taxi for you.
12. Do you believe in _____ justice for everybody?
13. Please would you put _____ rubbish out?
14. What about _____ beef for dinner?
15. Is _____ milk semi-skimmed or skimmed?
16. It seems that _____ mobiles are getting bigger rather than smaller!
17. Do you fancy _____ omelette?
18. Has _____ power come back on yet?
19. I didn't know that _____ dictionary belonged to you.
20. Have you eaten _____ chocolate from Grandma?

21. Both of us took _____ umbrella just in case.
22. We'll ask her for _____ information tomorrow.
23. There were _____ toys everywhere!
24. It's so important that you tell me _____ truth about them.
25. These are _____ channels that I watch most often.
26. He lived on _____ Porter Road when I used to know him.
27. Surprisingly, _____ unemployment had fallen again.
28. I need _____ new kettle, because this one is broken.
29. Can you bring me all _____ empty coffee cups, please?
30. You are _____ first person I have truly loved!

31. We'll be upset if he gets _____ infection.
32. Be careful! It's made of _____ glass.
33. How essential is _____ quality to you?
34. You need to replace _____ printer paper.
35. We start to develop _____ teeth when only a few months old.
36. She found _____ pen outside.
37. I don't like _____ peanut butter.
38. He was pleased with _____ poetry that he had written.
39. I told them about _____ Amanda.
40. Our swimming costumes were dry, but _____ children's weren't.

Test Your Grammar Skills

Which Article is Correct? 1

Complete the four gaps in each question with **a, an, the,** *and* **-** *(no article):*

1. - Have you seen **a)**_____ old jumper anywhere?

   - Is it **b)**_____ one with the blue collar?

   - Yes, and it's got **c)**_____ orange stripes.

   - It's over there, under **d)**_____ pile of cushions.

2. I went to **a)**_____ post office yesterday to post

   b)_____ parcel. It cost about **c)**_____

   twenty pounds, which I thought was **d)**_____ extortionate

   amount of money.

3. One of our neighbours is **a)**_____ guy who hails from

   b)_____ Finland. He is **c)**_____ interpreter

   who works at **d)**_____ same firm as my uncle.

4. - Let's put **a)**_____ kettle on and have

   b)_____ nice cup of tea.

   - Good idea! There's **c)**_____ open packet of chocolate

   biccies in the cupboard! What shall we drink to?

   - To **d)**_____ friendship!

Test Your Grammar Skills

Which Article is Correct? 2

*Complete the four gaps in each question with **a**, **an**, **the**, and **-** (no article):*

1. I haven't been to **a)**_____ work for fourteen days

   because I've had **b)**_____ really bad back. I got

   c)_____ awful pain at the base of my spine and

   d)_____ doctor told me that I had to rest.

2. - Shall we meet at **a)**_____ Burger King, or

   b)_____ new coffee house in Market Street?

   - They've got **c)**_____ offer on at the moment – if

   you buy **d)**_____ latte, you get two free mini doughnuts.

3. Geoffrey Chaucer was **a)**_____ English poet and

   philosopher who is considered by **b)**_____ scholars

   to be **c)**_____ greatest writer of the Middle Ages.

   The Canterbury Tales is **d)**_____ wonderfully rich piece

   of literature.

4. - Is there **a)**_____ free table anywhere in this café?

   - Yes, look – **b)**_____ table by the window is available.

   Oh – hang on – **c)**_____ old feller's just sat down.

   - Just our **d)**_____ luck!

Test Your Grammar Skills

Much, Many, Some, or Any? 1

*Complete each gap with **much**, **many**, **some**, or **any**:*

1. We didn't have _____ time to get to the concert.

2. I haven't got _____ sweets, but Sally has got _____ in her bag.

3. We're getting _____ better at kayaking!

4. I met _____ old friends at the restaurant yesterday.

5. Unlike _____ of his close friends, Paul had not had _____ opportunities in life.

6. How _____ courses are you taking this semester?

7. If we don't sell more clothes, there won't be _____ point in keeping this shop open.

8. Here's _____ money – go and buy as _____ tins of beans as you can.

9. Some of the children were vegetarian, so they didn't eat _____ meat.

10. If I hadn't eaten so _____ sweets, I wouldn't have needed _____ medication.

11. "How _____ homework have you got to do?" "Not _____."

12. Are there going to be _____ famous people at the party tonight?

13. Karl was _____ older than I had at first thought.

14. There have been too _____ reality shows on TV recently.

15. "Put some old clothes on and help me cut the grass." 'Which clothes?" "_____."

16. _____ days are _____ warmer than others around here.

17. There are _____ great reasons for learning English.

18. "Will there be _____ parking places?" "There might be _____."

19. I didn't have _____ to do yesterday, because there weren't _____ new clients to register.

20. This tree was planted _____ years ago by _____ of our forefathers.

Test Your Grammar Skills

Much, Many, Some, or Any? 2

*Correct the incorrect sentences using **much**, **many**, **some**, or **any**:*

1. Paula told Ian that there had been much rice in the jar that she had given him.

2. Many fans were dissatisfied with the result of the match on Saturday.

3. If we'd caught much fish in the competition yesterday, we could've had a barbecue!

4. How much would the cruise have cost us, if we'd got a discount?

5. Could you give me any advice about my job?

6. I've told you not to play in puddles so much times!

7. There was any carrot cake in the fridge last time I checked.

8. My daughter rejected much of the new clothes I bought her.

9. Is there any red paint left in that tub?

10. We did many great photography in the Western Desert last month.

11. It can be quite tough to learn some languages without a good teacher.

12. If you haven't got any wholemeal bread, I'll have a white sliced loaf, please.

13. Unfortunately, there were far too much students in my class this term.

14. We didn't enjoy the film that many, because we'd already watched it too many times.

15. Is there any reason why you're always late for choir practice, Barry?

16. If we had been able to move house, like we wanted to, we would've had many more space in the kitchen – and a garden.

17. To be honest, we hadn't been expecting any problems with our *brand new car!*

18. Mark fancied an ice cream, but he didn't have some money on him.

19. Some of the magazines were about fashion, while the others were about golf.

20. There's just too many apple juice in our cupboard!

Test Your Grammar Skills

Reported Speech Repartee – Bus Chat 1

Write each sentence using reported speech, e.g.

Bob: "The bus leaves at 2pm."   Bob said the bus left at 2pm.

1. Bob: "The bus usually comes at 4pm."   Bob said _____

2. Ellie: "The bus is coming."   Ellie replied _____

3. Bob: "The bus has arrived."   Bob stated _____

4. Ellie: "Some guys have been smoking." Ellie said _____

5. Bob: "The driver probably told them not to." Bob replied _____

6. Ellie: "The bus is moving slowly."   Ellie said _____

7. Bob: "We'll walk home tomorrow."   Bob said _____

8. Ellie: "Shall I open a window?"   Ellie asked _____

9. Bob: "You can if you want to."   Bob replied _____

10. Ellie: "I may go out tonight."   Ellie said _____

11. Bob: "I have to do my homework."   Bob replied _____

12. Ellie: "Yes, you ought to finish it." Ellie replied _____

13. Bob: "I didn't use to get so much."   Bob said _____

14. Ellie: "I know."   Ellie replied _____

15. Bob: "I will've finished it by 8 o'clock." Bob said _____

16. Ellie: "Do you want to meet up then?" Ellie asked _____

17. Bob: "I'll be meeting my girlfriend..." Bob said _____

18. Ellie: "I understand."   Ellie replied _____

19. Bob: "We arranged it last night."   Bob explained _____

20. Ellie: "This is my stop."   Ellie said _____

Test Your Grammar Skills

Reported Speech Repartee – Bus Chat 2

Write each sentence using reported speech, e.g.

Tom: "The bus is late."   Tom said the bus was late.

1. Tom: "I'm going to be late."   Tom said _____

2. Ira: "There are a lot of roadworks."   Ira said: _____

3. Tom: "Did you buy a paper?"   Tom asked _____

4. Ira: "It's in my bag."   Ira replied _____

5. Tom: "Can I have a look at it?"   Tom asked _____

6. Ira: "I've been reading it all afternoon."   Ira explained _____

7. Tom: "I'll read it while we're waiting."   Tom said _____

8. Ira: "Shall we have chips for tea?"   Ira suggested _____

9. Tom: "I would prefer egg on toast."   Tom stated _____

10. Ira: "I haven't got any bread."   Ira said _____

11. Tom: "Look at this picture!"   Tom told Ira _____

12. Ira: "I'm searching for my mobile."   Ira replied _____

13. Tom: "It's our neighbour, Mike Ball!" Tom said _____

14. Ira: "What's happened?"   Ira asked _____

15. Tom: "He was arrested last Tuesday."   Tom stated _____

16. Ira: "What's he done?"   Ira asked _____

17. Tom: "He was nicking flowerpots."   Tom replied _____

18. Ira: "Are you serious?"   Ira asked _____

19. Tom: "I was going to say that some   Tom said _____

    of ours have gone missing!"   _____

20. Ira: "Let's pay him a visit."   Ira suggested _____

Test Your Grammar Skills

100 Common Collocations with Get

get...

Literal Phrases:

angry about sth (become)
back (return)
the bus (take, catch)
Channel 5 (receive a TV or radio broadcast)
a cold (catch)
a criminal (catch, hold, apprehend)
a cup of tea (bring)
dinner (make, cook)
divorced (become)
sby to do sth (ask, persuade)
a doctor (call, request)
the door (answer)
dressed (become)
drunk (become)
excited (become)
a grade (achieve, earn, receive)
help (call for, ask)
home (return)
an idea (receive)
ill (become)
in (enter, e.g. a car)
some information (find out, discover, receive)
a job (find)
a letter (receive)
lost (become)
married (become)
some money (receive, earn)
a nappy (fetch)
a new book (buy, borrow)
off (disembark, e.g. bus, train, plane, etc.)
on (alight, e.g. bus, train, plane, etc.)
out (leave)
permission (ask, request, acquire)
the phone (answer)
pregnant (become)
a program (download, install)
punished (be)
ready (become)
a reward (receive)
rich (become)
a shower (have)
started (start, begin)
there (arrive)
through (contact, e.g. on the phone)
to sby (reach sby)
together (meet)
up (stand up, rise)
upset about sth (become)
used to sth (become)
wet (become)

Idioms:

about (travel frequently)
across (communicate)
your act together (improve your behaviour)
ahead (do better in life than other people)
at (suggest)
at sby (annoy sby, criticise)
away! (I don't believe you!)
away from (avoid)
away from it all (go on holiday)
sth back (have sth returned)
back to normal (return to a normal state)
sby's back up (annoy sby)
behind (support)
better (recover)
busy (become)
by (manage, esp. with little money)
cold feet (become unsure about doing sth)
down (become depressed)
down (dance)
down to sth (begin)
far (achieve a lot)
the hang of sth (learn how to do sth)
a head start (start sth before other people)
into sth (begin liking sth)
it (understand sth)
it in the neck (be told off)
a kick out of sth (enjoy, esp. sth negative)
a life (improve your life)
a load of sth (look at sth very interesting)
lost! (rude way to tell sby to leave)
the message (understand)
your money's worth (get a fair amount of sth)
a move on (hurry up)
moving (start)
nowhere (make no progress)
off on the wrong foot (start sth in a negative way)
on sby's nerves (annoy sby)
on with sby (have a good relationship)
out of sth (avoid doing sth unappealing)
sth out of sth (gain sth useful from a situation)
over sth (accept a negative situation, recover)
over yourself! (don't be so self-important)
people going (make people excited, tease)
rid of sth (dispose of)
the sack (lose your job)
somewhere (make progress)
through (survive, e.g. a difficult situation)
to (arrive, reach)
to sby (irritate sby)
told off (receive a verbal warning)

Test Your Grammar Skills

20 Different Meanings of Get

Get *is one of the most common verbs in English, with many different meanings – especially when you consider all the phrasal verbs and idioms that use it!*

Here are twenty different meanings of the verb **get**. *Match each one to a sentence below:*

achieve	become	catch	force	reach
annoy	bring	detain	pay	receive
answer	buy	earn	persuade	take
attack	call	experience	prepare	understand

1. I got the grade I needed for my assignment last week.

2. Can you get me a cup of tea please, love?

3. What time do you think they'll get home?

4. I'm sure things will get better in the end.

5. Mum will be getting dinner while I'm at swimming practice.

6. Don't worry – the police got the car thief red-handed.

7. "Don't worry about lunch – I'll get it." "Are you sure?" "Yes, it's on me."

8. Those bigger boys got Ben to give them his lunch money yesterday.

9. Tony will have to get the bus tomorrow, because his car is off the road.

10. Can you help me with this maths homework? I just don't get it.

11. We've got the suspect locked up in the cells downstairs.

12. We had to get the doctor out last night, because we were so worried about Roy.

13. Laura was running for the bus when she got a sudden pain in her foot.

14. "Why is your dog's leg bleeding?" "Another dog got him on the way home."

15. I got a really nice letter from my great grandma last week.

16. The fact that you don't listen gets me every time!

17. My mate's getting that new computer game from the shop later today.

18. I got my friend to join the new book club at the library.

19. I'm getting five pounds a week for looking after Mrs. Reynolds's cat.

20. Can you get the phone please – I'm busy!

Test Your Grammar Skills

Common Collocations with Get – 20 Phrasal Verbs

Get *is one of the most common verbs in English, with many different meanings – especially when you consider all the phrasal verbs and idioms that use it!*

Check that you know each phrasal verb, then write a sentence including each one, using the given times and forms:

	Verb:	Time:	Form:	
	get along	past	?	Why couldn't you both just get along?
1.	get back	past	+	_____
2.	get on with	future	-	_____
3.	get behind	past	?	_____
4.	get out of	pres.	+	_____
5.	get at	past	-	_____
6.	get to	future	?	_____
7.	get out	past	+	_____
8.	get on	pres.	-	_____
9.	get up to	past	?	_____
10.	get by	future	+	_____
11.	get together	past	-	_____
12.	get off	pres.	?	_____
13.	get down to	past	+	_____
14.	get through	future	-	_____
15.	get round to	past	?	_____
16.	get into	pres.	+	_____
17.	get over	past	-	_____
18.	get up	future	?	_____
19.	get through to	past	+	_____
20.	get away from	pres.	-	_____

Test Your Grammar Skills

Common Collocations with Get – 20 Idioms

Get *is one of the most common verbs in English, with many different meanings – especially when you consider all the phrasal verbs and idioms that use it!*

Check that you know each phrasal verb, then write a sentence including each one, using the given times and forms:

Verb:	Time:	Form:	
get the sack	past	?	Why did Katie get the sack yesterday?

1. get stuck into — pres. — + — _____
2. get away with sth — future — - — _____
3. get it in the neck — past — ? — _____
4. get away from it all — future — + — _____
5. get somebody's point — pres. — - — _____
6. get your money's worth — future — ? — _____
7. get along with sby — past — + — _____
8. get cold feet — future — - — _____
9. get on sby's nerves — pres. — ? — _____
10. get nowhere — future — + — _____
11. get into sth — past — - — _____
12. get lost — future — ? — _____
13. get away! — pres. — + — _____
14. get your act together — future — - — _____
15. get to somebody — past — ? — _____
16. get a feel for sth — future — + — _____
17. get a life — pres. — - — _____
18. get a move on — future — ? — _____
19. get a kick out of sth — past — + — _____
20. get a head start — future — - — _____

Test Your Grammar Skills

100 Common Collocations with Make and Do

MAKE	*Translation:*	DO	*Translation:*
amends	_____	40 miles an hour	_____
an application	_____	an assignment	_____
appointment	_____	business	_____
an arrangement	_____	the cleaning	_____
the bed	_____	a course	_____
believe	_____	a crossword	_____
the best of something	_____	some damage	_____
a cake	_____	a dance	_____
certain	_____	the dirty on sby	_____
a change	_____	somebody's dirty work	_____
a choice	_____	the dishes	_____
a comment	_____	your duty	_____
a cup of tea	_____	an exam	_____
a decision	_____	some exercise	_____
a difference	_____	somebody a favour	_____
dinner	_____	the gardening	_____
a discovery	_____	good	_____
do	_____	your hair	_____
an effort	_____	some harm	_____
ends meet	_____	your homework	_____
an excuse	_____	the honours	_____
eyes at somebody	_____	the housework	_____
a face	_____	the ironing	_____
a fool of yourself	_____	justice to something	_____
friends	_____	the laundry	_____
fun of somebody	_____	more harm than good	_____
a fuss	_____	your nails	_____
history	_____	nothing	_____
light of	_____	one	_____
a list	_____	some paperwork	_____
a mess	_____	some research	_____
a mistake	_____	right	_____
a model	_____	the shopping	_____
money	_____	something	_____
a noise	_____	something crazy	_____
an observation	_____	sth out of character	_____
an offer	_____	sth unexpected	_____
a payment	_____	time	_____
a phone call	_____	too much	_____
a prediction	_____	the trick	_____
progress	_____	the washing	_____
a promise	_____	the washing up	_____
a reservation	_____	well	_____
sense	_____	some work	_____
something of yourself	_____	wrong	_____
a speech	_____	you good	_____
a suggestion	_____	your best	_____
sure	_____	your own thing	_____
waves	_____	yourself proud	_____
your mind up	_____	your worst	_____

Test Your Grammar Skills

Make or Do – Common Collocations 1

Complete each gap below with either **make** *or* **do**:

1. _____ a bet
2. _____ a job
3. _____ the dishes
4. _____ a skirt
5. _____ the cleaning
6. _____ your hair
7. _____ believe
8. _____ amends
9. _____ some damage
10. _____ an offer
11. _____ fifty press ups
12. _____ some yoghurt
13. _____ a fortune
14. _____ yourself proud
15. _____ a noise
16. _____ your best
17. _____ the washing up
18. _____ an application
19. _____ some work
20. _____ some harm

21. _____ a favour
22. _____ a man of you
23. _____ a profit
24. _____ an error
25. _____ the washing
26. _____ your nails
27. _____ do
28. _____ well in something
29. _____ a promise
30. _____ some practice
31. _____ a reservation
32. _____ a mess
33. _____ your duty
34. _____ ends meet
35. _____ an effort
36. _____ your own thing
37. _____ an enquiry
38. _____ some money
39. _____ waves
40. _____ eyes at someone

Test Your Grammar Skills

Make or Do – Common Collocations 2

Complete each gap below with either **make** *or* **do***:*

1. _____ the laundry
2. _____ an appearance
3. _____ something crazy
4. _____ a phone call
5. _____ a fuss
6. _____ your worst
7. _____ laws
8. _____ the big time
9. _____ the honours
10. _____ something great
11. _____ an excuse
12. _____ an appointment
13. _____ 40 miles per hour
14. _____ sense
15. _____ sure of something
16. _____ your way home
17. _____ an exam
18. _____ a fire
19. _____ a face
20. _____ a decision

21. _____ business with someone
22. _____ a date
23. _____ a fool of someone
24. _____ justice to something
25. _____ an impression
26. _____ an incision
27. _____ more harm than good
28. _____ too much
29. _____ a speech
30. _____ the grade
31. _____ really well at maths
32. _____ a suggestion
33. _____ a crossword
34. _____ a prediction
35. _____ the shopping
36. _____ history
37. _____ some exercise
38. _____ the trick
39. _____ somebody's dirty work
40. _____ a mistake

Test Your Grammar Skills

Make or Do – Common Collocations (Gap-Fill)

Complete each gap with either **make** *or* **do** *in an appropriate form:*

1. We _____ about 100 miles an hour when the cops caught up with us.

2. If you would like _____ an application, we will consider it along with the rest.

3. Can you put the paint down please! Just look at the mess you _____!

4. Ella _____ the ironing all morning before her stepmum got home.

5. So I fitted a new fan belt and it looks like that _____ the trick.

6. I phoned you because I wanted _____ sure you were alright, Grandma.

7. The twins _____ the shopping for the party in town this morning.

8. I wish that dog would be quiet! He _____ a racket all night!

9. Could you _____ me a favour and lend me twenty quid till Tuesday please?

10. At the end of the volunteering holiday, we all felt that we _____ a big difference.

11. If you _____ the dishes, I can get on the phone and _____ the hotel reservation.

12. If Shelley _____ her nails properly, her friend wouldn't _____ fun of her.

13. I _____ the crossword by the time you get back from the chemist.

14. Lucy always _____ excuses for not _____ her bed.

15. It _____ you good to go out for a brisk walk by the sea.

16. If Owen breaks the world record for the fourth time he _____ history!

17. You have to _____ a choice: _____ the housework or _____ me a coffee!

18. Paul _____ a phone call to Jeff, because he wanted to _____ him an offer for his car.

19. Alfie _____ fifty minutes of piano practice last night.

20. If you try _____ her apologise, I'm sure it _____ more harm than good.

Test Your Grammar Skills

Mistakes that English Native Speakers Make 1

Believe it or not, English native speakers sometimes make mistakes when using their own language! To find them, simply read a daily newspaper regularly or check out some of the leaflets at an English Tourist Information Centre or library! Identify <u>one</u> mistake in each sentence below and write the letter of the category that it belongs to out of the following:

A. apostrophes   B. articles   C. capital letters
D. clumsy style   E. commas   F. extra or missing words
G. spelling mistakes

1. Keep the kid's brains active during the holidays with our great summer school!

2. Are you fed up with reading about others good fortune?

3. Newcastle, it is clear is a city of great contrasts.

4. I had told the papers that I didn't had want to talk to them, but they still followed me.

5. We can go by car, or it's about twenty minutes walk from here.

6. We were glad that the councillors were able to stay did for the whole afternoon.

7. When you see our prices you won't beleive your eyes!

8. The children's play train is now boarding. Get on borad!

9. An umbrella that stays up when it gets windy – what an great idea!

10. Are you going out on New Years Eve?

11. Thinking of learning to hang-glide? You'll soon ge the hang of it!

12. The station is only about thirty-five minutes drive away.

13. Adult tikets – £4.60.

14. We are aiming to improve individual's skills with our new computer courses.

15. Children will be able compete in four different age categories.

16. Make Someone happy Today – Smile!

17. If things aren't going well, why not advise yourself of a new course of action?

18. We're all really looking forward to the wedding on October 8th!!!!

19. Our products offer solutions to a range of every day IT and wireless communication needs.

20. We are working hard to improve our store so that it will be without question, the best hardware store in the city.

Test Your Grammar Skills

Mistakes that English Native Speakers Make 2

Believe it or not, English native speakers sometimes make mistakes when using their own language! To find them, simply read a daily newspaper regularly or check out some of the leaflets at an English Tourist Information Centre or library! Identify <u>one</u> mistake in each sentence below and write the letter of the category that it belongs to out of the following:

A. apostrophes   B. articles   C. capital letters
D. clumsy style   E. commas   F. extra or missing words
G. spelling mistakes

1. Its worth asking about our amazing offers!

2. This ticket is valid for any friday or Saturday in December.

3. A few months a go I was earning £650 per month for 30 hours per week. Since then my salary has doubled.

4. Have you read Bridget Jones Diary?

5. Jennifer Jameson, our accountant is due to retire at the end of next month.

6. Do you know how many Eurpean countries have signed up to the single currency?

7. He's a spy, a con-man, a lover, and a theif. Now he's back for a new adventure!

8. The new Ford Focus is in a different class from all the former ones which have gone before it.

9. You are welcome to join us in church for a Easter celebration.

10. The information about Richard and Tina's originated from reliable sources.

11. Every monday night is party night at McCoy's.

12. Become a teaching assistant and make a real difference to a childs life.

13. You can find us on St. Johns Street, near the post office.

14. Children under 8 years old must be with accompanied by an adult.

15. SALE! Robbie William's latest album is half-price for a limited time only.

16. We will be open allday on Sunday.

17. Our stores are now open everyday of the week.

18. You are what you et, or so they say.

19. Half of the managers were the proposals and half were against. It was an even split.

20. This car has got the lot – Style, speed, and a dazzling array of extras.

Test Your Grammar Skills

Mistakes that English Native Speakers Make 3

Believe it or not, English native speakers sometimes make mistakes when using their own language! To find them, simply read a daily newspaper regularly or check out some of the leaflets at an English Tourist Information Centre or library! Identify <u>one</u> mistake in each sentence below and write the letter of the category that it belongs to out of the following:

A. apostrophes   B. articles   C. capital letters
D. clumsy style   E. commas   F. extra or missing words
G. spelling mistakes

1. Packaging design is sooooooo important! An eye-catching design can make all the difference to the number of products sold.

2. Can you book the room a few days' before you plan to come?

3. Special offer – get up to 12 months half price line rental on all feature phones.

4. Kojak's hair Salon – open Monday to Saturday. Late opening on Wednesdays.

5. So many poeple enjoy the peaceful scenery at Sandcastle Gardens.

6. For more details about any of our products, please contact laura on 01332 442 5900.

7. If you would like to hire a tennis court please a member of staff.

8. Its sale time at Harrington's Department Store!

9. Computer printer cartridges will be on offer throughout the month on of June.

10. Do your children spend every weekend pouring over their school books?

11. All of the people on the committee will have to come of attend the annual meeting.

12. I haven't seen my family since last Christmas's Eve.

13. I need at least two days notice if you want to come with me to Birmingham.

14. The office of Allen's Solicitors has recently been refurbished, so there shouldn't be anymore building work in the foreseeable future.

15. We would like to welcome you to our latest catalogue0.

16. What are your New Years resolutions?

17. The plane left on schedule but, unbelievably we were still late arriving in Singapore.

18. We are now booking for new year's eve.

19. Our company is offering an new opportunity for school leavers.

20. I'm really looking forward next month to getting a new karaoke machine.

Test Your Grammar Skills

Mistakes that English Native Speakers Make 4

Believe it or not, English native speakers sometimes make mistakes when using their own language! To find them, simply read a daily newspaper regularly or check out some of the leaflets at an English Tourist Information Centre or library! Identify <u>one</u> mistake in each sentence below and write the letter of the category that it belongs to out of the following:

A. apostrophes   B. articles   C. capital letters
D. clumsy style   E. commas   F. extra or missing words
G. spelling mistakes

1. We offer the best deal in town on tyres and exausts.

2. An impolite tortoise can make its owners life a misery.

3. Its' only £5.99 per person for three games of bowling.

4. The deputy manager, who is on holiday will deal with your enquiry very soon.

5. Coming soon – "A Midsummer's Night Dream".

6. The 15.15 train service to Leicester has been canceled.

7. Come to the Old King's Head and enjoy a 3-course meal for only £8.99. At the Old Kings Head we pride ourselves on the quality of our service.

8. Paulo's – a no.1 Italian restaurant in the Greater London area.

9. John and Jenny Lewis' family-run hotel is an enchanting place to stay.

10. This years school concert will have something for everyone.

11. See you in an hours time.

12. We will be closed for business from Friday 14th May until Tuesday 18th May. If you have got anything you want to ring us about you can give us a ring on…

13. The date when a library book is due back is stamped on a first page of the book.

14. For the best deals in town – get down to mark's bargain basement.

15. Come and visit Mrs. Johnsons Tea Rooms (turn left after the bridge).

16. If you would like to apply for the vacansy, please email your CV to…

17. Have you tried Harvey's Bistro yet?!!

18. If you wait, the receptionist will arrange a appointment for you.

19. "Nico's Business Tips" is a new programme especially just for would-be tycoons.

20. Please make all cheques payable to mr. Phil Sanders.

Test Your Grammar Skills

Polite, Neutral, or Rude Language 1

Read the situations below and decide which type of language is most likely to be used – polite, neutral, or rude. Compare the different responses and consider why they may or may not be appropriate:

Situation 1   **Receiving a certificate from the Dean of your university:**

a) Polite: "Thank you very much."

b) Neutral: "Thanks. That's great."

c) Rude: "Thanks for nothing. This place is a dump. I'm so glad I'm leaving. I'll never be coming back!"

Situation 2   **Renting a DVD at the video shop:**

a) Polite: "Excuse me, madam. I don't mean to be rude, but I was wondering whether you possibly have *The Lego Movie* available for home rental?"

b) Neutral: "Hi. Have you got *The Lego Movie*?"

c) Rude: "Where's *The Lego Movie*?"

Situation 3   **At a job interview:**

a) Polite: "I am very interested in the job, because I enjoy working in a customer service environment and meeting new people."

b) Neutral: "I haven't worked for a while, so I'm just looking for something to keep me going really. I don't mind what."

c) Rude: "Look – are you going to give me the job or not? Because I'm really busy and I don't want to sit around here all day. And open the window! It's so hot in here."

Situation 4   **Somebody in another car drives into the back of your car at the traffic lights:**

a) Polite: "Good morning, sir. Lovely day, isn't it? Would you mind awfully removing your four-wheel-drive from the back of my Corsa?"

b) Neutral: "Oh dear. Look at the mess. Oh. I don't know what to do. We'll have to swap insurance details."

c) Rude: "You stupid idiot! What on earth are you doing? I don't believe it! What were you thinking? For goodness' sake – you went right into the back of me!"

Test Your Grammar Skills

Polite, Neutral, or Rude Language 2

Read the situations below and decide which type of language is <u>most likely</u> to be used – polite, neutral, or rude. Compare the different responses and consider why they may or may not be appropriate:

Situation 5   **Complaining to your manager about a new work colleague:**

a) Polite: "I just wanted to have a little word with you about one of our more recently employed colleagues, a Mr. Anthony R. Brown. We have found ourselves in something of a disagreement regarding the utilisation of space within our shared working environment."

b) Neutral: "Can I have a word with you about Anthony? He's started using my desk without asking me first."

c) Rude: "That new guy has nicked my desk! It's bang out of order! I had a go at him about it yesterday. You're the manager – you're supposed to sort these things out, not just stand there gurning like an imbecile."

Situation 6   **Asking for a loan at the bank:**

a) Polite: "We'd like to apply for about ten thousand pounds, if that's possible."

b) Neutral: "We're going to need about ten grand, I would think."

c) Rude: "Give us the money or we'll be taking our business somewhere that appreciates us!"

Situation 7   **Asking when the next bus is due:**

a) Polite: "I wonder, dear sir, if you could perhaps find your way towards informing me as to whether there is a bus due to be arriving where we are now standing, within a suitably short period of time?"

b) Neutral: "Excuse me, do you know whether there's a bus due soon?"

c) Rude: "Can you get out of the way? You're blocking the bus timetable, you fat fool."

Situation 8   **Thanking your elderly grandmother for the expensive birthday present that she has sent you:**

a) Polite: "Thank you so much for the earrings. They are absolutely wonderful. It was so kind of you to think of me. You really shouldn't have, grandma!"

b) Neutral: "Thanks for the earrings. They're nice."

c) Rude: "Is that all I'm getting this year? You're so mean – and you're getting worse!"

Test Your Grammar Skills

Polite, Neutral, or Rude Language 3

Read the situations below and decide which type of language is most likely to be used – polite, neutral, or rude. Compare the different responses and consider why they may or may not be appropriate:

Situation 9 **Buying a train ticket:**

a) Polite: "Please would you be so kind as to sell me a ticket which will allow me to make a return journey to the fine city of Newcastle-upon-Tyne today? I shall remain forever in your debt."

b) Neutral: "I'd like a day return to Newcastle, please. I've got a railcard."

c) Rude: "Give me a ticket for Newcastle. Return? Of course I want a return. I'm not going to stay there indefinitely, am I? How stupid can you get?"

Situation 10 **You are in the pub with your friends, when a stranger accidentally spills your drink:**

a) Polite: "Oh my goodness! I see that there has been an unfortunate mishap. Allow me to help you mop up the spillage."

b) Neutral: "Oops. Oh dear. Can you get a towel from the bar to help me clear it up? Thanks."

c) Rude: "You've ruined my trousers! You idiot! Don't just stand there gawping at me – go and get some towels or something from the bar!"

Situation 11 **You are in the park, when you see some boys throwing rocks at swans:**

a) Polite: "I really don't think you should be doing that, do you? Now run along, there's good boys."

b) Neutral: "Er, stop that..."

c) Rude: "Hey! Stop it! What do you think you're doing? Pack it in! Clear off!"

Situation 12 **Asking a friend if they want to go to the cinema:**

a) Polite: "Would it be an enormous inconvenience if you were to attend the cinema with me this evening, at a time which will be arranged so as to be mutually agreeable to the both of us?"

b) Neutral: "Do you want to go to the cinema later?"

c) Rude: "Liam is busy so I suppose I've got no choice – I'll have to go to the cinema with you. You're paying. And you can get me some popcorn too. A big tub."

Test Your Grammar Skills

Polite, Neutral, or Rude Language 4

Read the situations below and decide which type of language is <u>most likely</u> to be used – polite, neutral, or rude. Compare the different responses and consider why they may or may not be appropriate:

Situation 13 **While out shopping someone with a clipboard stops you and asks you to make a donation to their charity:**

a) Polite: "Thank you so much for this marvellous and unprecedented opportunity to give to your charitable fund, but unfortunately I am rather late for an incredibly important appointment, so I must now hurry along. Please do forgive me for being unable to spend some moments of quality time speaking with you."

b) Neutral: "Sorry, I can't stop now. I'm in a bit of a rush."

c) Rude: "Get out of my way. Can't you see I'm busy? You can stop waving your clipboard at me – I haven't got any money! Why don't you get a proper job anyway?"

Situation 14 **Asking a friend if they will spend two days of their holiday helping you to move house:**

a) Polite: "Would you mind possibly helping me to move next week? I'm really sorry about the timing because I know that you're supposed to be on holiday but I would really appreciate it, if that's OK."

b) Neutral: "Will you help me move house next week?"

c) Rude: "To be honest, you're the last person I would trust to be handling any of my valuable belongings, but I'm completely stuck because absolutely no one else is available. I've tried asking my real friends, and they're all busy next week, so I'm reduced to asking you."

Situation 15 **You find out that your partner is having a relationship with someone else:**

a) Polite: "Oh dear, that is rather a shock. Well, I'm sorry that I have evidently been a cause of unhappiness and disappointment to you and hope that you will both be very happy together. Farewell then, darling. I'll see myself out."

b) Neutral: "Well, how long has it been going on? Yes, I'm a bit stunned. How serious is it?"

c) Rude: "I knew you were trouble from the moment I set eyes on you! I should never have trusted you in the first place. You can give me back my CDs and all my DVDs! And all the stuff I've bought you – including the diamond engagement ring! Now get out of my house. Get out! OUT!"

Test Your Grammar Skills

100 Great English Oxymorons – Phrases that Contradict Themselves!

absolutely unsure
accurate estimate
active retirement
act naturally
advanced beginner
all alone
almost always
awfully nice
bad health
bad luck
boxing ring
calculated risk
civil disobedience
civil war
classic rock & roll
clean toilet
clear as mud
cold sweat
common courtesy
completely destroyed
conservative liberal
consistently inconsistent
controlled chaos
criminal justice
crisis management
critical acclaim
deafening silence
definite maybe
eloquent silence
essential luxury
fatally injured
foreign national
free credit
friendly fire
genuine imitation
graduate student
great depression
group of individuals
half full
home office
homework
humanitarian invasion
ill health
incomplete cure
incredibly dull
initial conclusion
intense apathy
last initial
limited freedom
liquid gas

lower inflation
minor disaster
minor miracle
modern history
never again
new tradition
non-alcoholic beer
non-working mother
nothing much
numbing sensation
one hundred and ten percent
one size fits all
only choice
open secret
organised chaos
original copy
partially completed
passive aggressive
peacekeeping force
perfectly normal
permanent substitute
personal computer
practice test
pretty ugly
pure 100% orange juice from concentrate
real polyester
recent past
relative stranger
required donation
resident alien
retired worker
safe bet
safety hazard
same difference
school holiday
science fiction
second best
seriously funny
short distance
single copy
social outcast
student teacher
think out loud
toll free
tough love
unbiased opinion
unfunny joke
virtual reality
working party
young adult

Test Your Grammar Skills

Match English Oxymorons – An Extract from a Novel

Check the meaning of each oxymoron, then complete the gaps in the story below:

safety hazard	perfectly normal	act naturally
awfully nice	tough love	bad luck
school holiday	student teacher	all alone
same difference	social outcast	relative stranger
completely destroyed	common courtesy	open secret
absolutely unsure	foreign national	incredibly dull
unbiased opinion	deafening silence	recent past
modern history	numbing sensation	accurate estimate
young adult	intense apathy	non-alcoholic beer
eloquent silence	group of individuals	safe bet

"We met some guys in the pub last night, who at first seemed 1._____. One of them, a former sniper called László, began telling us about a bit of 2._____ he'd been having recently. I noticed he was downing 3._____ and I listened to his story more out of 4._____ than anything else.

"He said that he was a Hungarian 5._____ who had been raised by his strict hard-working parents with 6._____. As a 7._____ his father had been a 8._____ working at a 9._____ college. One 10._____ he took László for a long drive in their car, which was a bit of a 11._____, because it didn't have any indicators. Anyway, as this 12._____ yakked on, I could see his pals were mocking him behind his back. It appeared to be an 13._____ that László's tales concerning his 14._____ were nothing more than a complete fabrication.

"I tried to 15._____, but to be honest I was 16._____ what to do, since any comments I was able to make were met with a 17._____. It was the 18._____ to me whether László's words were factual or not, but the 19._____ around him looked on with 20._____ expressions and an air of 21._____. It became clear that László was a bit of a 22._____, without any genuine confidants, and it was a 23._____ that his supposed friends had been nothing more than mere hangers-on.

"This turned out to be an 24._____, because after another half an hour or more of the sniper's tall tales about his apparently vital role in 25._____, his companions had melted away into the half-darkness one by one, until at last László sat silently before us, 26._____. Sometimes an 27._____ is more rewarding than a lengthy exchange, and I believe that László could feel this too, although he seemed crestfallen, his confidence perhaps 28._____. As we ordered another round of drinks and finally got to know facets of the real László, he calmed down and the strange 29._____ which had dogged me for most of the evening began to disperse. It really had been, in my 30._____, a most unusual night."

Answers to Worksheets and Notes for Use

Part One

9   1. yesterday (past continuous). 2. tomorrow (future perfect). 3. every day (present simple). 4. yesterday (past perfect). 5. at the moment (present continuous). 6. tomorrow (future simple). 7. today (present perfect). 8. Every day (present simple). 9. at the moment (present continuous). 10. today (present perfect continuous). 11. tomorrow (future continuous). 12. yesterday (past perfect continuous). 13. yesterday (past simple). 14. every day (present simple). 15. tomorrow (future with 'going to').

10   1. every day (present simple). 2. tomorrow (future simple). 3. yesterday (past perfect). 4. tomorrow (future with 'going to'). 5. at the moment (present continuous). 6. today (present perfect). 7. every day (present simple). 8. at the moment / tomorrow (present continuous). 9. today (present perfect continuous). 10. yesterday (past perfect continuous). 11. tomorrow (future perfect). 12. yesterday (past continuous). 13. tomorrow (present simple). 14. tomorrow (future simple). 15. yesterday (past simple).

11   Answers will vary. Sample answers: 1. Paul was making pizza in the kitchen. / Paul isn't making pizza in the kitchen. / Will Paul be making pizza in the kitchen tomorrow? 2. My aunt wasn't watching a film at the cinema. / Is my aunt watching a film at the cinema? / My aunt will be watching a film at the cinema. 3. Was Terri adding a friend to her phonebook? / Terri is adding a friend to her phonebook. / Terri won't be adding a friend to her phonebook. 4. Harriet was spending some time at the beach yesterday afternoon. / Harriet is not spending some time at the beach. / Will Harriet be spending some time at the beach tomorrow afternoon? 5. Her brother wasn't driving to Leicester yesterday morning. / Is her brother driving to Leicester on Friday morning? / Her brother will be driving to Leicester tomorrow morning.

12   Answers will vary. Sample answers: 1. Her father was learning Italian at the community centre. / Her father isn't learning Italian at the community centre any more. / Will her father be learning Italian at the community centre next term? 2. You weren't looking at photos all afternoon. / Are you looking at photos tomorrow afternoon? / You will be looking at photos this afternoon. 3. Was Kerri ordering chairs for her client last week? / Kerri is ordering chairs for her client. / Kerri won't be ordering chairs for her client. 4. Annabel was waiting for her colleague near the cathedral for two hours. / Annabel isn't waiting for her colleague near the cathedral. / Will Annabel be waiting for her colleague near the cathedral tomorrow afternoon? 5. Tom wasn't putting milk in his coffee. / Is Tom putting milk in his coffee? / Tom will be putting milk in his coffee.

13   A) 1. watering. 2. washing / drying. 3. writing. 4. watching. 5. clearing. 6. doing. 7. feeding. 8. staring. 9. trying on. 10. chatting. 11. putting. 12. knitting. 13. sitting. 14. washing / drying. 15. visiting. 16. having. 17. waiting. 18. reading. 19. playing. 20. throwing. B) Answers will vary.

14   Answers will vary. Sample answers: 1. Alison had already told her manager about her holiday. / Alison hasn't told her manager about her holiday. / Will Alison have told her manager about her holiday by the time she goes? 2. My son hadn't been to the golf club that morning. / Has your son been to the golf club this morning? / My son will have been to the golf club by the time you get back. 3. Had Charlie taken his dog to

Answers to Worksheets and Notes for Use

the vet's before he went to work? / Charlie has just taken his dog to the vet's. / Charlie will not have taken his dog to the vet by then. 4. We had hung the painting in the hall. / We haven't hung the painting in the hall. / Will we have hung the painting in the hall before Emma arrives? 5. Simon hadn't lost much weight that month. / Has Simon lost much weight this month? / Simon will have lost a lot of weight by the time we next meet.

15 Answers will vary. Sample answers: 1. Kevin had cleaned the sink with disinfectant. / Kevin hasn't cleaned the sink with disinfectant. / Will Kevin have cleaned the sink with disinfectant by lunchtime? 2. She hadn't made any curtains for the living room. / Has she made the curtains for the living room yet? / She will've made the curtains for the living room by the end of May. 3. Had they received an email from the hotel before they left home? / They have received an email from the hotel today. / They won't have received an email from the hotel by tomorrow. 4. The tourists had asked the waiter for directions. / The tourists haven't asked the waiter for directions. / Will the tourists have asked the waiter for directions before they finish their meal? 5. Sheila's boyfriend hadn't run ten miles on Sunday afternoon. / Has Sheila's boyfriend run ten miles this morning? / Sheila's boyfriend will have run ten miles by the time you finish your breakfast.

16 Answers will vary. Sample answers: A) How long has Jean been doing her homework for? For twenty minutes. Has Jean been doing her homework for twenty minutes? Yes, she has. Has Jean been doing her homework for half an hour? No, she hasn't. Jean hasn't been doing her homework for half an hour.

Extensions:
Who has been doing their homework for twenty minutes? Jean has. etc.
What has Jean been doing for twenty minutes? Her homework. etc.
Whose homework has Jean been doing for twenty minutes? *Her* homework. etc.

B) Where has your book group been meeting since 2004? In this cafe. Has your book group been meeting in this cafe since 2004? Yes, it has. Has your book group been meeting in a pub since 2004? No, it hasn't. Our book group hasn't been meeting in a pub since 2004.

Extensions:
How long has your book group been meeting in this cafe? Since 2004. etc.
Whose book group has been meeting in this cafe since 2004? Our book group has. etc.
Which book group has been meeting in this cafe since 2004? Our book group has. etc.
What has your book group been doing since 2004? Meeting in this cafe. etc.

17 Answers will vary. Sample answers: A) Why were you waiting outside your house for an hour? Because I had lost my key. Were you waiting outside your house for an hour, because you had lost your key? Yes, I was. Were you waiting outside your house for an hour, because you like being outside? No, I wasn't. I wasn't waiting outside my house for an hour, because I like being outside.

Extensions:
What were you doing outside your house for an hour, because you had lost your key? Waiting. etc.

Answers to Worksheets and Notes for Use

Who was waiting outside your house for an hour, because they had lost their key? I was. etc.

Where were you waiting for an hour, because you had lost your key? Outside my house. etc.

How long were you waiting outside your house, because you had lost your key? For an hour. etc.

B) When were Melanie and Steve tidying their kitchen cupboards? All morning. Were Melanie and Steve tidying their kitchen cupboards all morning? Yes, they were. Were Melanie and Steve tidying their kitchen cupboards yesterday evening? No, they weren't. Melanie and Steve were not tidying their kitchen cupboards yesterday evening.

Extensions:

What were Melanie and Steve tidying all morning? Their kitchen cupboards. etc.

What were Melanie and Steve doing all morning? Tidying their kitchen cupboards. etc.

Who were tidying their kitchen cupboards all morning? Melanie and Steve (were). etc.

Whose kitchen cupboards were Melanie and Steve tidying all morning? Their kitchen cupboards. etc.

How long were Melanie and Steve tidying their kitchen cupboards? All morning. etc.

Which cupboards were Melanie and Steve tidying all morning? Their kitchen cupboards. etc.

18   Answers will vary. Sample answers: A) Who had eaten the last ginger biscuit to make Jack angry? Harry (had). Had Harry eaten the last ginger biscuit to make Jack angry? Yes, he had. Had Pauline eaten the last ginger biscuit to make Jack angry? No, she hadn't. Pauline hadn't eaten the last ginger biscuit to make Jack angry.

Extensions:

What had Harry eaten to make Jack angry? The last ginger biscuit. etc.

What had Harry done to make Jack angry? (He had) eaten the last ginger biscuit. etc.

Which biscuit had Harry eaten to make Jack angry? The last ginger biscuit. etc.

What kind of biscuit had Harry eaten to make Jack angry? The last *ginger* biscuit. etc.

Why had Harry eaten the last ginger biscuit? To make Jack angry. etc.

B) When had the delivery van arrived? Before Mike got back from work. Had the delivery van arrived before Mike got back from work? Yes, it had. Had the delivery van arrived the day before? No, it hadn't. The delivery van hadn't arrived the day before.

Extensions:

What had the delivery van done before Mike got back from work? (It had) arrived. etc.

What had happened before Mike got back from work? The delivery van had arrived. etc.

Which van had arrived before Mike got back from work? The delivery van. etc.

What kind of van had arrived before Mike got back from work? The delivery van. etc.

Answers to Worksheets and Notes for Use

19   Answers will vary. Sample answers: A) Why had you been jogging for an hour and a half? As part of our training programme. Had you been jogging for an hour and a half as part of your training programme? Yes, we had. Had you been jogging for an hour and a half for fun? No, we hadn't. We hadn't been jogging for an hour and a half for fun.

Extensions:
What had you been doing for an hour and a half as part of your training programme? Jogging. etc.
Who had been jogging for an hour and a half as part of your training programme? We had. etc.
How long had you been jogging as part of your training programme? For an hour and a half. etc.

B) Which team had been working on the project for months, before making their final breakthrough? The senior team. Had the senior team been working on the project for months, before making their final breakthrough? Yes, it had. Had the junior team been working on the project for months, before making their final breakthrough? No, it hadn't. The junior team hadn't been working on the project for months, before making their final breakthrough.

Extensions:
Who had been working on the project for months, before making their final breakthrough? The senior team. etc.
What had the senior team been working on for months, before making their final breakthrough? The project. etc.
What had the senior team been doing for months, before making their final breakthrough? Working on the project. etc.
How long had the senior team been working on the project, before making their final breakthrough? For months. etc.

20   Answers will vary. Sample answers: A) When will mum be waiting for me in the corridor? After school. Will mum be waiting for me in the corridor after school? Yes, she will. Will mum be waiting for me in the corridor at lunchtime? No, she won't. Mum won't be waiting for you in the corridor at lunchtime.

Extensions:
Who will be waiting for me in the corridor after school? Mum will. etc.
Who will mum be waiting for in the corridor after school? You. etc.
Where will mum be waiting for me after school? In the corridor. etc.
What will mum be doing after school? Waiting for you in the corridor. etc.

B) What will you be presenting during the meeting? A series of challenging questions. Will you be presenting a series of challenging questions during the meeting? Yes, I will. Will you be presenting a series of humorous anecdotes during the meeting? No, I won't. I won't be presenting a series of humorous anecdotes during the meeting.

Extensions:
When will you be presenting a series of challenging questions? During the meeting. etc.

Answers to Worksheets and Notes for Use

Who will be presenting a series of challenging questions during the meeting? I will. etc.

What will you be presenting during the meeting? A series of challenging questions. etc.

What will you be doing during the meeting? Presenting a series of challenging questions. etc.

What kind of questions will you be presenting during the meeting. A series of challenging questions. etc.

21   Answers will vary. Sample answers: A) How long will Thomas and Anna have been married for on Friday? (For) ten years. Will Thomas and Anna have been married for ten years on Friday? Yes, they will (have). Will Thomas and Anna have been married for eight years on Friday? No, they will not (have). Thomas and Anna will not have been married for eight years on Friday.

Extensions:
Who will have been married for ten years on Friday? Thomas and Anna will (have). etc.
When will Thomas and Anna have been married for ten years? On Friday. etc.

B) What will you have ordered, by the time I get to the restaurant? My main course. Will you have ordered your main course, by the time I get to the restaurant? Yes, I will (have). Will you have ordered your dessert, by the time I get to the restaurant? No, I won't (have). I won't have ordered my dessert, by the time you get to the restaurant.

Extensions:
Which course will you have ordered, by the time I get to the restaurant? My main course. etc.
What will you have done, by the time I get to the restaurant? Ordered my main course. etc.
When will you have ordered your main course (by)? By the time you get to the restaurant. etc.
Who will have ordered their main course, by the time I get to the restaurant? I will. etc.

22   1. could've, should've, would've. 2. would've, could've, should've. 3. would've, should've, could've. 4. should've, would've, could've. 5. could've, would've, should've. 6. would've, should've, could've. 7. could've, would've, should've. 8. should've, could've, would've. 9. could've, would've, should've. 10. could've, would've, should've.

23   1. should've, would've, could've. 2. could've, would've, should've. 3. should've, could've, would've. 4. could've, would've, should've. 5. should've, could've, would've. 6. would've, should've, could've. 7. should've, would've, could've. 8. should've, would've, could've. 9. would've, could've, should've. 10. would've, could've, should've.

Answers to Worksheets and Notes for Use

24   1)

infinitive	s form	past tense	past participle	ing form
bumble around	bumbles around	bumbled around	bumbled around	bumbling around
buzz off	buzzes off	buzzed off	buzzed off	buzzing off
catch up with	catches up with	caught up with	caught up with	catching up with
come over	comes over	came over	come over	coming over
drive off	drives off	drove off	driven off	driving off
drop off	drops off	dropped off	dropped off	dropping off
fall over	falls over	fell over	fallen over	falling over
get off	gets off	got off	got off	getting off
hurry up	hurries off	hurried off	hurried off	hurrying off
keel over	keels over	keeled over	keeled over	keeling over
keep up with	keeps up with	kept up with	kept up with	keeping up with
melt away	melts away	melted away	melted away	melting away
pass by	passes by	passed by	passed by	passing by
pop round	pops round	popped round	popped round	popping round
queue up	queues up	queued up	queued up	queueing up
roll around	rolls around	rolled around	rolled around	rolling around
sidle up	sidles up	sidled up	sidled up	sidling up
topple over	topples over	toppled over	toppled over	toppling over
turn up	turns up	turned up	turned up	turning up
walk off	walks off	walked off	walked off	walking off

2) a) & b) Answers will vary. Sample answers:

Infinitive: pop round   Tense: past simple

+ Hannah's friend popped round to see her yesterday.

- Hannah's friend didn't pop round to see her yesterday.

? Did Hannah's friend pop round to see her yesterday?

Answers to Worksheets and Notes for Use

25 1)

infinitive	s form	past tense	past participle	ing form
agree with	agrees with	agreed with	agreed with	agreeing with
answer back	answers back	answered back	answered back	answering back
blurt out	blurts out	blurted out	blurted out	blurting out
chime in with	chimes in with	chimed in with	chimed in with	chiming in with
disagree with	disagrees with	disagreed with	disagreed with	disagreeing with
drone on	drones on	droned on	droned on	droning on
fob off	fobs off	fobbed off	fobbed off	fobbing off
get across	gets across	got across	got across	getting across
gloss over	glosses over	glossed over	glossed over	glossing over
hang up	hangs up	hung up	hung up	hanging up
joke around	jokes around	joked around	joked around	joking around
mouth off	mouths off	mouthed off	mouthed off	mouthing off
open up	opens up	opened up	opened up	opening up
point out	points out	pointed out	pointed out	pointing out
quieten down	quietens down	quietened down	quietened down	quietening down
rabbit on	rabbits on	rabbited on	rabbited on	rabbiting on
report back to	reports back to	reported back to	reported back to	reporting back to
speak out	speaks out	spoke out	spoken out	speaking out
tell off	tells off	told off	told off	telling off
write down	writes down	wrote down	written down	writing down

2) a) & b) Answers will vary. Sample answers:

Infinitive: drone on   Tense: past continuous

+ The teacher was droning on about phrasal verbs for ages yesterday.

- The teacher wasn't droning on about phrasal verbs for ages yesterday.

? Was the teacher droning on about phrasal verbs for ages yesterday?

26   Answers will vary. Sample answers: 1. I will **bring** you a sandwich later. 2. You weren't **working** very hard today, were you? 3. Is he **feeling** better today? 4. She has been **spending** time with her sister this afternoon. 5. We didn't **put** the butter back in the fridge – Roger did. 6. Will they have **helped** with preparations by the time the event begins? 7. If I **get** to work early, I have time for a cup of coffee. 8. If you don't **finish** your homework in time, you will get in trouble. 9. Does he **mean** what he said about quitting college? 10. She's **living** in Las Vegas at the moment. 11. If we hadn't **joined** the gym, we wouldn't have improved our fitness. 12. Will they have been **baking** all morning? 13. I had **asked** my friend about a lift to the airport a few times. 14. Unfortunately, you are not going to **meet** the President tomorrow morning. 15. Had he been **visiting** the museum when the rain began? 16. She has **known** Tom since 1994. 17. We will not be **running** in the marathon tomorrow. 18. Did they **hear** the news about Katie's gap year last night? 19. If I **played** netball for my country, I would feel really proud. 20. You haven't been **listening** to me.

Answers to Worksheets and Notes for Use

31 1. false. 2. false. 3. true. 4. false. 5. false. 6. true. 7. false. 8. true. 9. true.
10. true. 11. false. 12. false. 13. true. 14. true. 15. true. 16. false. 17. true.
18. false. 19. false. 20. true.

32-36 Tenses Revision Game: The aim of this game is to promote better understanding of the features and uses of the five basic tenses in English: Present Simple, Present Continuous, Past Simple, Present Perfect, and Future Simple. Each page has twelve cards with features and uses of one tense. Method: cut up all the cards and mix them up, e.g. in a box. T (teacher) designates an area of the classroom for each of the five tenses – e.g. five different tables. SS (students) work in small groups. Each group gets an equal number of cards. SS have to move around the classroom putting each card in the correct place, e.g. the card with 'regular time' on it would go on the 'Present Simple' table, and so on. T monitors and gives help as required. T can check understanding by getting into short discussions with SS, asking why they have put a particular card with a particular tense – and encouraging them to think again, if it was the wrong choice. T monitors the timing of the activity, which could last between 10-20 minutes, with longer time being allowed for lower-level groups. SS should learn about the five tenses in an active way, being allowed by T to discover the information themselves through group discussion, rather than simply being given it on a handout. SS should end up with all the cards being with the correct tense, and could be given a copy of pp.27 and 29 for reference – or write out the information in a table. T should note which areas SS got wrong, so that they can be addressed in future lessons. A different approach would be to focus on a particular tense with T eliciting from SS the information about time, form, auxiliary verbs, etc. with examples on the board.

37 Answers will vary. Sample answers: 1. Mike plays golf with his mates twice a week. 2. If Mike plays golf with his mates twice a week, he feels great. 3. Mike is playing golf with his mates at the moment. 4. Mike has played golf with his mates this week. 5. Mike has been playing golf with his mates today. 6. Play golf with your mates! 7. Mike played golf with his mates yesterday. 8. Mike was playing golf with his mates last week. 9. Mike had played golf with his mates before he went to work. 10. Mike had been playing golf with his mates for four hours. 11. If Mike had played golf with his mates earlier, he would have felt better. 12. Mike will play golf with his mates later. 13. Mike will be playing golf with his mates tomorrow at 9am. 14. Mike is going to play golf with his mates later today. 15. If Mike plays golf with his mates today, he won't play tomorrow. 16. If Mike played golf with his mates every day, he would become really good! 17. Mike will have played golf with his mates by this time tomorrow. 18. Mike will have been playing golf with his mates for two hours, by the time you get there tomorrow.

If you did all the extension activities, you could write up to 12 sentences for each tense (where possible), making a maximum of 216 sentences. For example:

Present Simple: Mike plays golf with his mates twice a week.

Extension 1:
Negative form: Mike does not play golf with his mates twice a week.
Question (yes/no): Does Mike play golf with his mates twice a week?

Extension 2:
Reported Speech: He said Mike played golf with his mates twice a week.
He said Mike did not play golf with his mates twice a week.

Answers to Worksheets and Notes for Use

He asked whether Mike played golf with his mates twice a week.

Extension 3:
Passive Voice:

Golf is played (by Mike with his mates) twice a week.
Golf is not played (by Mike with his mates) twice a week.
Is golf played (by Mike with his mates) twice a week?

Extension 4:
Passive Voice in
Reported Speech:

He said golf was played (by Mike with his mates) twice a week.
He said golf was not played (by Mike with his mates) twice a week.
He asked whether golf was played (by Mike with his mates) twice a week.

38   Answers will vary. Sample answers: 1. I walk in the garden every day. 2. If I walk in the garden every day, it is good for my health. 3. I am walking in the garden at the moment. 4. I have walked in the garden this week. 5. I have been walking in the garden today. 6. Walk in the garden! 7. I walked in the garden yesterday. 8. I was walking in the garden last week. 9. I had walked in the garden before breakfast. 10. I had been walking in the garden for twenty minutes. 11. If I had walked in the garden last night, I would have seen a shooting star. 12. I will walk in the garden later. 13. I will be walking in the garden tomorrow at 10.30am. 14. I'm going to walk in the garden later today. 15. If I walk in the garden, I will get wet feet. 16. If I walked in the garden every day, I would feel relaxed. 17. I will have walked in the garden by this time tomorrow. 18. I will have been walking in the garden for ten minutes, by the time you arrive.

If you did all the extension activities, you could write up to 12 sentences for each tense (where possible), making a maximum of 216 sentences. For example:

Past Simple:

I walked in the garden yesterday.

Extension 1:
Negative form:
Question (yes/no):

I didn't walk in the garden yesterday.
Did you walk in the garden yesterday?

Extension 2:
Reported Speech:

She said she had walked in the garden yesterday.
She said she had not walked in the garden yesterday.
She asked whether I had walked in the garden yesterday.

Extension 3:
Passive Voice:

Not possible. We are very unlikely to say:
"The garden was walked in (by me) yesterday."

Extension 4:
Passive Voice in
Reported Speech:

Not possible.

Answers to Worksheets and Notes for Use

Part Two

40 1. loathed. 2. keep. 3. are lying. 4. lasts. 5. 've been thinking. 6. saw. 7. don't fit. 8. 're having. 9. seemed, does he want. 10. have. 11. has been promising. 12. consists of, put. 13. were weighing. 14. realise. 15. were being.

41 1. can't hear. 2. love, did it cost. 3. are involving. 4. didn't recognise. 5. were driving. 6. don't mind. 7. were relying on, were. 8. Do you fancy, sounds. 9. 'm defrosting. 10. doesn't matter. 11. doesn't believe in. 12. were tasting. 13. Do you own. 14. agree. 15. had been wishing, notice.

43 1. Has Mary been playing the piano all afternoon? 2. Have they been going to the same campsite for nearly twelve years? 3. Have Roger and his brother been asking their friends for donations? 4. Has your teacher been talking for the past half an hour? 5. Have you been reading about whales and dolphins this morning? 6. Have Peter's parents been staying with him since Saturday? 7. Have you been making a birthday cake for your brother's party? *or* Have you been making a cake for your brother's birthday party? 8. Have the newspaper reporters been bothering you today? 9. Has Jason been talking about me? 10. Has her little dog been running around outside all day?

44 1. Was the train leaving just as you arrived? 2. Were you going into the kitchen when the phone rang? 3. Were you reading funny posts on Twitter most of the night? 4. Were you thinking of inviting my mother to Tim's birthday meal? 5. Was the bee buzzing around in an annoying manner yesterday? 6. Were you always making up in-jokes about Kevin? 7. Was your uncle running a bath when the earthquake began? 8. Were the children refusing to eat their salad when grandma arrived? 9. Was the meteorite heading straight for earth when it exploded? 10. Was Lena's husband going to meet his son from a former marriage?

45 1. Had you switched off all the lights before going to bed? 2. Had Jeremy lived in Cromer Road since 1989? 3. Had the pupils completed their work before going out to play? 4. Had John already left by the time you got home? *or* Had you already left by the time John got home? 5. Had somebody drunk half your drink when you returned from the bathroom? 6. Had Liam made a phone call by the time his boss appeared? 7. Had you ever considered a career as a chef while still at school? 8. Had your parents just gone to bed last night when you phoned them? 9. Had you already seen that movie? 10. Had you already bought the meat before you found out that the party had been cancelled?

46 1. Had you been waiting for me to arrive before starting the meeting? 2. Had it been raining the day before your holiday ended? 3. Had Philip been painting the garage all morning? 4. Had you both been playing Monopoly every Monday for four years? 5. Had the suspect been running for about twenty minutes when you caught him? 6. Had you been working at the florist's since Easter when you got promoted? 7. Had you been meaning to tell me about the broken microwave? 8. Had Jessica been hoping to catch an earlier flight? 9. Had you been playing games on your tablet before you went out? 10. Had you already been discussing the possibility of cancelling your holiday, before Tom brought it up yesterday? *or* Had Tom already

Answers to Worksheets and Notes for Use

been discussing the possibility of cancelling your holiday, before you brought it up yesterday?

47 1. Will you be getting a taxi home this evening? 2. Will Sue be reading a book in the library at two o'clock tomorrow afternoon? 3. Will you be helping me at the craft fair next week? 4. Will you be thinking about me while I'm having my exam later? 5. Will Richard be travelling to the meeting at 6pm tomorrow? 6. Will you be bringing your friends to the party on Tuesday? 7. Will we be landing in a few minutes? 8. Will Steven be collecting money while the group does their dance? 9. Will the government be spending more time listening to voters this year? 10. Will all the shops be opening late again this Christmas?

48 1. Will you have gone to bed by the time I get back? 2. Will Terry have finished his project by the end of next week? 3. Will Jamie have scored the most goals by the end of the season? 4. Will you have cashed up by the time the restaurant closes? 5. Will Trudie have tidied her room before the film starts? 6. Will the computer engineer have fixed the problem by one o'clock? 7. Will you have waited for more than twenty minutes by the time the bus arrives? 8. Will you have got a new hairstyle by the time I see you again? 9. Will the best seats have sold out by the time I get through to the ticket shop? 10. Will our snowman have melted by the time Grandpa gets to see it?

49 1. will she? 2. mustn't he? 3. can't it? 4. can you? 5. will we? 6. must she? 7. can't she? 8. won't they? 9. won't we? 10. must we? 11. will she? 12. can we? 13. must I? 14. can we? 15. can't he? 16. won't it? 17. mustn't it? 18. can't they? 19. mustn't you? 20. can't you?

50 1. shouldn't you? 2. couldn't they? 3. should you? 4. wouldn't you? 5. could I? 6. shouldn't he? 7. could it? 8. would it? 9. could we? 10. shouldn't they? 11. couldn't she? 12. wouldn't we? 13. shouldn't it? 14. could we? 15. should they? 16. could you? 17. should she? 18. couldn't they? 19. shouldn't we? 20. would he?

53 Instructions: you are involved in helping to organise your school variety show. You are at a meeting to discuss who will do each job at the variety show. Use **future simple passive** to write full sentences stating who is *scheduled* to do what, e.g.

1. a) SHOW > **DIRECT** > BEN (MR. BRAHMS) The show will be directed by Ben.

But when the day of the variety show finally arrived, absolutely nothing went to plan! The person in brackets ended up doing the job in question, so write a sentence using **past simple (active voice)** to show what actually happened:

1. b) Mr. Brahms directed the show.

Then write a sentence using **past simple passive** that you can put in your after-show report:

1. c) The show was directed by Mr. Brahms.

In summary, you have to write three sentences for each question:

i)   passive voice with future simple

Answers to Worksheets and Notes for Use

ii)   active voice with past simple
iii)   passive voice with past simple

Note: each group of three sentences could also be drilled orally.

Extension: students could write similar sets of sentences about a real event that happened at their school.

Answers: 1. a) The show will be directed by Ben. b) Mr. Brahms directed the show. c) The show was directed by Mr. Brahms. 2. a) The songs will be composed and sung by Alison Watts. b) Megan Watts composed and sang the songs. c) The songs were composed and sung by Megan Watts. 3. a) The script will be written by Graham. b) Gok wrote the script. c) The script was written by Gok. 4. a) The costumes will be made by Barbara's mother. b) Mrs. Parsons and her team made the costumes. c) The costumes were made by Mrs. Parsons and her team. 5. a) The set will be built by Tom and Ben. b) Mr. Arthur and Big Dan built the set. c) The set was built by Mr. Arthur and Big Dan. 6. a) The sketches will be performed by The Peterson Twins. b) Carly and Ben performed the sketches. c) The sketches were performed by Carly and Ben. 7. a) The sound will be operated by Mike B. b) Gordon operated the sound. c) The sound was operated by Gordon. 8. a) The stage will be swept by Carly's cousin. b) Big Dan swept the stage. c) The stage was swept by Big Dan. 9. a) The programmes will be printed by the school secretary. b) Tom's dad printed the programmes. c) The programmes were printed by Tom's dad. 10. a) The chairs will be put out by Owen and Mac. b) The school secretary put out the chairs. c) The chairs were put out by the school secretary. 11. a) The venue will be booked by Mr. Brahms. b) Louise Hudd booked the venue. c) The venue was booked by Louise Hudd. 12. a) The make-up will be done by Sandra's mother and Mrs. Whelk. b) Olive did the make-up. c) The make-up was done by Olive. 13. a) The event will be filmed for DVD by Jocelyn Whispers. b) Silver Screen Productions filmed the event for DVD. c) The event was filmed for DVD by Silver Screen Productions. 14. a) The coffees and teas will be made by Mrs. Parsons and her team. b) Mr. Parsons and his team made the coffees and teas. c) The coffees and teas were made by Mr. Parsons and his team. 15. a) The piano will be played by Gok. b) Mike B. played the piano. c) The piano was played by Mike B. 16. a) The curtain will be raised and lowered by Big Dan. b) Little Dan raised and lowered the curtain. c) The curtain was raised and lowered by Little Dan. 17. a) The dance sequences will be choreographed by Louise Hudd. b) Gok choreographed the dance sequences. c) The dance sequences were choreographed by Gok. 18. a) The scenery will be painted by Mr. Arthur and Big Dan. b) The Peterson Twins painted the scenery. c) The scenery was painted by the Peterson Twins. 19. a) The show will be sponsored by Glover Insurance. b) Global Travel sponsored the show. c) The show was sponsored by Global Travel. 20. a) The props will be provided by Carly's Uncle Clive. b) Louise's dad provided the props. c) The props were provided by Louise's dad.

54   1. breaks down. 2. has broken up. 3. will have given away. 4. checked out. 5. was falling behind. 6. has been tidying up. 7. did up. 8. will chat up. 9. were picking on. 10. brighten up. 11. has grown up. 12. were putting up. 13. keep up with. 14. nod off. 15. came across. 16. cheer up. 17. mix up. 18. get over. 19. held on. 20. fell over.

Answers to Worksheets and Notes for Use

55 1. throw away. 2. let, down. 3. will have set off. 4. has been swotting up on. 5. were working out. 6. will have been looking after. 7. told off. 8. will be slogging away. 9. 've thought about. 10. make up. 11. held up. 12. log out of. 13. walked in on. 14. zip up. 15. will take over. 16. turned up. 17. pipe down. 18. was slowing down. 19. put up with. 20. has been leaving out.

56 Note for pages 56-57: you could make these pages easier by removing the obligation to write two clauses, or by using easier tenses.

Answers will vary. Sample answers: 1. Will put across his message by talking directly into the camera. 2. If Linda puts away the dishes, I usually give her an extra scoop of ice cream. 3. We're putting by twenty pounds every month to pay for your school trip to Prague next year. 4. I've put down my book and I'm waiting to have a chat with you. 5. The boss has been putting his son down for years, because he doesn't rate him as a businessman. 6. Put forward two possible candidates for the election – one could be progressive and the other more conservative. 7. Tania's parents were put through a lot of unnecessary stress because of her rebellious nature. 8. I was putting in a lot of extra hours at work, but I didn't get any overtime pay. 9. Caroline had put a lot of effort into winning the contract, but she wasn't fairly rewarded. 10. They had been putting off cleaning out the garage for ages, but yesterday they finally got round to it. 11. If we had put back the meeting to the following month, everybody would have been much more prepared. 12. Will you put on that new dress I bought you, so that I can see whether it fits? 13. Tim will be putting out the bins just before the rubbish collection tomorrow. 14. I hope it isn't going to put you out too much to collect me from the airport tonight. 15. If you put the proposal to David now, he'll have all morning to consider it. 16. If we put together both of our incomes, we'd all be better off. 17. We will have put a hundred pounds towards your charity appeal by the end of this month. 18. By next month, we will have been putting guests up in our B&B for exactly twenty years. 19. If I could drive, I would have put my transport problems behind me. 20. Vernon put up with criticism from his wife, because he loved her very much.

57 Answers will vary. Sample answers: 1. Why does your friend always come with you to this class, when he isn't interested in Physics? 2. If you come across well at interviews, you have a better chance of getting a job. 3. My jacket is coming apart at the seams, so I'll have to get it repaired. 4. We have come away from the conference with lots of good ideas for teaching English. 5. A professional clown has been coming into this school to teach circus skills for the past six weeks. 6. Come back, Sean! I haven't finished talking yet! 7. All the rowing about money had come between them, and Andy and Geri were considering a trial separation. 8. My parents phoned to say they were coming by for a cup of tea, but unfortunately we were out. 9. If I came round tomorrow, could I borrow a large saucepan, please? 10. Agricultural labourers had been coming from the valleys to the town in search of work for years, before the factory was built. 11. If you hadn't come in just after I'd gone out, we could have had a night in together. 12. I think unless we try to glue the broom handle back on, it'll come off when we use it again. 13. I'm sure that Larry will be coming out with plenty of witty one-liners when he gives his best man's speech on Friday. 14. Al is going to come over and study with us later, so try not to embarrass me too much, OK? 15. If our relatives come down from Scotland for the New Year's do, we'll have a great laugh! 16. If Mike hadn't come out of the shop when he did, he wouldn't have bumped into Mandy. 17. By the end of term, almost every student will have come together to help decorate the new library. 18. The scriptwriters came up with a lot of

Answers to Worksheets and Notes for Use

great ideas, but we couldn't use them all. 19. If I were more relaxed, I wouldn't have come up against so many problems with my colleagues. 20. There's just one thing that I don't understand – how did this mess come about?

59 1. to give. 2. taking. 3. privatising. 4. stealing. 5. eating. 6. to help. 7. meeting. 8. smoking. 9. *either* to sit *or* sitting. 10. to go. 11. hiring. 12. to read. 13. to buy. 14. lending. 15. to eat out. 16. playing. 17. *either* to read *or* reading. 18. *either* to visit *or* visiting. 19. to be. 20. to dance. **Hate**, **like**, and **prefer** can be followed by either gerund or infinitive.

60 1. asking. 2. *either* to fall *or* falling. 3. to sell. 4. to do. 5. trying. 6. to collect. 7. to take. 8. missing. 9. to invite. 10. *either* to buy *or* buying. 11. to go. 12. marking. 13. to receive. 14. to change. 15. spending. 16. to be. 17. wearing. 18. to find. 19. to buy. 20. taking. **Begin** and **continue** can be followed by either gerund or infinitive.

61 1. annoying. 2. skiing. 3. calling. 4. preparing. 5. upsetting. 6. wanting. 7. telling. 8. working. 9. holidaying. 10. paying. 11. training. 12. stealing. 13. standing. 14. falsifying. 15. going. 16. meeting. 17. sleeping. 18. covering. 19. worrying. 20. reminiscing. 21. getting. 22. smoking. 23. bowling. 24. fishing. 25. living. 26. losing. 27. kicking. 28. sleeping. 29. talking. 30. taking.

62 1. collecting. 2. finishing. 3. finding. 4. drinking. 5. having. 6. taking. 7. beating. 8. getting. 9. waiting. 10. seeing. 11. swimming. 12. Learning. 13. messing. 14. driving, walking. 15. shopping. 16. watching. 17. being. 18. spending. 19. remembering. 20. damaging. 21. attending. 22. making. 23. losing. 24. flying, catching. 25. upsetting. 26. going. 27. ordering. 28. looking. 29. Dancing. 30. buying.

Part Three

64 Note for pages 64-67: once an activity has been completed, SS could cut up the cards and mix them up for another group of students to put back into order.

Answers will vary. Sample answers: 1. Frankie. 2. piano. 3. got. 4. home. 5. profits. 6. all afternoon. 7. Alyson. 8. her assignments. 9. bumped into. 10. in the entrance. 11. four paintings. 12. by the end of this week. 13. Jack. 14. his coursework. 15. placed. 16. in a cardboard box. 17. for you. 18. at 6pm. 19. Laura. 20. a great job offer.

65 Answers will vary. Sample answers: 1. Terry. 2. spag bol and fries. 3. have tried on. 4. in Miss Selfridge. 5. naughty words. 6. throughout the lesson. 7. The thieves. 8. a priceless antique vase. 9. will get. 10. from the grocery store. 11. on bikes. 12. for over an hour. 13. Mr Timms. 14. money. 15. has been looking. 16. in the park. 17. a few ready meals. 18. by now. 19. Bianca. 20. a facial.

Answers to Worksheets and Notes for Use

66 Answers will vary. Sample answers:

	Subject:	Verb:	Object:	Place:	Time:
1.	The postman	ate	an apple	in the park	last Wednesday.
2.	Carla	has had	a massage	at the spa	today.
3.	The flatmates	are going to buy	a new fridge	for their house	tomorrow.
4.	Des	was writing down	the answers	in the exam hall	yesterday.
5.	Our cat	ripped up	a £50 cardigan	in the kitchen	last week.
6.	Scientists	will have found	intelligent life	in the universe	by 2250.
7.	Lola	is admiring	a painting	in the gallery	at the moment.
8.	Ben	parked	his 4X4	at the market	on Friday lunchtime.
9.	Simon	is going to make	some ice cream	at Lily's flat	later on.
10.	The manager	will be dealing with	any issues	in her office	at quarter past four.

67 Answers will vary. Sample answers:

	Subject:	Verb:	Object:	Place:	Time:
1.	Mrs. Jenkins	received	a few phone calls	at home	this morning.
2.	The girls	have been writing	Christmas cards	in the study	all afternoon.
3.	Theo's Donuts	announced	a new kind of filling	at a press conference	last week.
4.	Jemima	rides	quad bikes	in the old quarry	every Monday evening.
5.	Their toddler	was making	funny faces	in the restaurant	the whole time.
6.	The orchestra	had taken	a break	in the refectory	before restarting.
7.	The music app	will be downloading	the whole album	to the SIM card	while you are asleep.
8.	Our parents	will've been leading	nature walks	along remote coastal paths	for four days, by the time you arrive.
9.	Old Grandpa	has produced	some wonderful cider	in his 'secret' brewery	these past few years.
10.	Wallace	is unpacking	his clothes	in his tiny tent	now.

68 A. ancient (4), glass (7), huge (2), short (2), youthful (4), leather (7), dreadful (1), business (8), rectangular (3), book (8), Irish (6), splendid (1), cream (5), spherical (8), northern (6), maroon (5). Write 4 more adjectives: answers will vary.
B. Answers will vary.

69 1. interesting old newspaper. 2. major new TV. 3. yummy freshly-made apple. 4. splendid blue and white cotton. 5. miniature Estonian painted. 6. unpleasant skinny young. 7. majestic rocky mountain. 8. curved red Victorian. 9. long bumpy dirt. 10. ugly old brown. 11. slim 18-year-old Spanish. 12. exclusive Mexican beach. 13. cuddly furry teddy. 14. astonishing new techno. 15. extra-large cotton work. 16. offbeat short comedy. 17. difficult long-distance. 18. magical Christmas sleigh. 19. large roomy living. 20. unusual ancient Mayan.

70 Answers will vary. Sample answers: 1. a) and hurried to work. b) but it didn't matter because it's the weekend! c) I was out last night. d) so I didn't have time for breakfast. 2. a) or snowing. b) even though the forecast predicted it would. c) and I walked to work instead of driving. d) but he still took his umbrella just in case. 3. a) and made a speech thanking his team. b) whereas his teammate came third. c) because he had trained exceptionally hard. d) so he was selected to run for the county. 4. a) even though it wasn't due until Friday. b) so let's go out for a meal. c) whereas my brother has to wait two more days. c) and I'm ready to go shopping! 5. a) or take a taxi. b) even though we own a car. c) because neither of us can drive. d) but always walk to the shopping mall. 6. a) rather than tomorrow morning. b) or

Answers to Worksheets and Notes for Use

next Tuesday. c) even though we don't really want to see them. d) so we need to prepare our proposal. 7. a) or I won't be able to call Jenny. b) rather than using your phone. c) because I need to send a text to Joe. d) even though I have to go out right now! 8. a) rather than simply upset. b) but the councillors still wouldn't listen to us. c) whereas the teacher remained relatively calm. d) so the restaurant manager offered to give us 10% off the bill.

71 Answers will vary. Sample answers: 1. a) even though Liz had paid for fast delivery. b) whereas the letter got there on time. c) because Sam hadn't posted it straight away. d) so Gina complained to the Post Office. 2. a) but when we got there it was closed. b) and parked outside the main entrance. c) rather than getting the bus. d) even though it's only five minutes' walk from home. 3. a) or glass, please? b) because I need to make a cup of tea. c) so that James can have a coffee? d) rather than a plate? 4. a) or I won't mark it. b) but you can keep in most of this paragraph. c) even though it wasn't that bad. d) because it was completely illegible. 5. a) and I don't care who knows it. b) or if not, he had a lot to do with it. c) rather than Sammy's, as we had previously thought. d) whereas he wanted us to think it wasn't. 6. a) rather than buying one at the supermarket. b) but then I dropped it on the floor! c) even though we'd only just finished the last one. d) but nobody wanted to try it. 7. a) and so have I. b) so she'll have to ask the teacher for an extension. c) whereas I handed in my work two weeks ago. d) because her father has been in hospital. 8. a) so don't offer him anything else. b) and I don't think he should eat any more. c) or if he hasn't, you could offer him a sandwich. d) whereas I will be absolutely famished!

73

	Article:	Noun:	Type of Noun:	Rule:
a)	-	music	uncountable – abstract / general	8
b)	the	employees	plural / specific	5
c)	the	time	singular countable / specific	3
d)	-	chewing gum	uncountable – concrete / general	6
e)	a	film	singular countable / general / consonant sound	1
f)	-	Paris	proper	10
g)	an	app	singular countable / general / vowel sound	2
h)	-	cakes	plural / general	4
i)	the	potato	singular countable / specific	3
j)	-	Coca-Cola	proper	10
k)	the	progress	uncountable – abstract / specific	9
l)	a	car	singular countable / general / consonant sound	1
m)	the	rice	uncountable – concrete / specific	7
n)	-	children	plural / general	4
o)	an	egg	singular countable / general / vowel sound	2
p)	the	patience	uncountable – abstract / specific	9
q)	the	socks	plural / specific	5
r)	the	money	uncountable – concrete / specific	7
s)	-	perseverance	uncountable – abstract / general	8
t)	-	hair	uncountable – concrete / general	6

Answers to Worksheets and Notes for Use

74

	Article:	Noun:	Type of Noun:	Rule:
a)	the	grass	uncountable – concrete / specific	7
b)	-	Darren	proper	10
c)	-	ice cream	uncountable – concrete / general	6
d)	the	pen	singular countable / specific	3
e)	-	work	uncountable – abstract / general	8
f)	an	orange	singular countable / general / vowel sound	2
g)	the	photo	singular countable / specific	3
h)	the	dedication	uncountable – abstract / specific	9
i)	-	students	plural / general	4
j)	-	Tuesday	proper	10
k)	-	petrol	uncountable – concrete / general	6
l)	the	courage	uncountable – abstract / specific	9
m)	-	life	uncountable – abstract / general	8
n)	a	coat	singular countable / general / consonant sound	1
o)	-	colds	plural / general	4
p)	an	idea	singular countable / general / vowel sound	2
q)	the	furniture	uncountable – concrete / specific	7
r)	the	assignments	plural / specific	5
s)	a	book	singular countable / general / consonant sound	1
t)	the	chips	plural / specific	5

75
1. - . 2. - . 3. - . 4. the. 5. - . 6. the. 7. the. 8. an. 9. the. 10. a. 11. a. 12. - . 13. the. 14. - . 15. the. 16. - . 17. an. 18. the. 19. the. 20. the. 21. an. 22. - . 23. - . 24. the. 25. the. 26. - . 27. - . 28. a. 29. the. 30. the. 31. an. 32. - . 33. - . 34. the. 35. - . 36. a. 37. - . 38. the. 39. -. 40. the.

76
1. a) an. b) the. c) - . d) a. 2. a) the. b) a. c) - . d) an. 3. a) a. b) - . c) an. d) the. 4. a) the. b) a. c) an. d) - .

77
1. a) - . b) a. c) an. d) the. 2. a) - . b) the. c) an. d) a. 3. a) an. b) - . c) the. d) a. 4. a) a. b) the. c) an. d) - .

78
1. much. 2. any, some. 3. much. 4. some. 5. some, many. 6. many. 7. any. 8. some, many. 9. much. 10. many, any. 11. much, much. 12. any. 13. much. 14. many. 15. Any. 16. Some, much. 17. many. 18. any, some. 19. much, many. 20. many, some.

79
1. Paula told Ian that there had been **some** rice in the jar that she had given him. 2. Correct. 3. If we'd caught **some/many** fish in the competition yesterday, we could've had a barbecue! 4. Correct. 5. Could you give me **some** advice about my job? 6. I've told you not to play in puddles so **many** times! 7. There was **some** carrot cake in the fridge last time I checked. 8. My daughter rejected **some/many** of the new clothes I bought her. 9. Correct. 10. We did **some** great photography in the Western Desert last month. 11. Correct. 12. Correct. 13. Unfortunately, there were far too **many** students in my class this term. 14. We didn't enjoy the film that **much**, because we'd already watched it too many times. 15. Correct. 16. If we had been able to move house, like we wanted to, we would've had **much** more space in the kitchen – and a garden. 17. Correct. 18. Mark fancied an ice cream, but he didn't have **much/any** money on him. 19. Correct. 20. There's just too **much** apple juice in our cupboard!

Answers to Worksheets and Notes for Use

80   1. the bus usually came at 4pm. 2. that the bus was coming. 3. that the bus had arrived. 4. some guys had been smoking. 5. the driver had probably told them not to. 6. the bus was moving slowly. 7. they would walk home the following day. 8. whether she should open a window. 9. that she could if she wanted to. 10. she might go out that night. 11. that he had to do his homework. 12. that he ought to finish it. 13. that he didn't use to get so much. 14. that she knew. 15. he would have finished it by 8 o'clock. 16. whether he wanted to meet up then. 17. he would be meeting his girlfriend. 18. that she understood. 19. that they had arranged it the previous night. 20. that was her stop.

81   1. he was going to be late. 2. there were a lot of roadworks. 3. whether Ira had bought a paper. 4. that it was in her bag. 5. whether he could have a look at it. 6. that she had been reading it all afternoon. 7. he would read it while they were waiting. 8. they had chips for tea. 9. that he would prefer egg on toast. 10. she hadn't got any bread. 11. to look at a picture. 12. that she was searching for her mobile. 13. it was their neighbour, Mike Ball. 14. what had happened. 15. that he had been arrested the previous Tuesday. 16. what he had done. 17. that he had been nicking flowerpots. 18. whether Tom was serious. 19. that he had been going to say that some of theirs had gone missing. 20. paying him a visit. / that they should pay him a visit.

83   1. achieve. 2. bring. 3. reach. 4. become. 5. prepare. 6. catch. 7. pay. 8. force. 9. take. 10. understand. 11. detain. 12. call. 13. experience. 14. attack. 15. receive. 16. annoy. 17. buy. 18. persuade. 19. earn. 20. answer.

84   Answers will vary. Sample answers: 1. I had to get back to work by ten o'clock. 2. I won't be getting on with the housework, because Carl is coming round. 3. Did you get behind with your schoolwork when you were ill? 4. I get out of bed at six o'clock every morning. 5. I wasn't getting at you yesterday; I just wanted to make sure you were alright. 6. What time will we get to Oklahoma? 7. The news got out that Annie was leaving Malcolm. 8. Our parents are not getting on very well at the moment. 9. What did you get up to during your vacation? 10. I'll be able to get by in college without your help. 11. They used to get together every two months, but now it's only once a year. 12. Are you getting off at this stop? 13. The meeting began and we got down to business. 14. I won't get through this revision without you! 15. Did you get round to picking up my dry cleaning? 16. Ally is getting into the car at the moment. 17. It wasn't easy for Samantha to get over the death of her beloved goldfish. 18. Are we getting up early on Monday morning? 19. After ringing him a few times, I finally got through to Mark. 20. You can't get away from the fact that it's your turn to do the washing up!

85   Answers will vary. Sample answers: 1. I always love getting stuck into a new project. 2. You won't get away with this kind of behaviour! 3. Did Sally get it in the neck when she got home late last night? 4. We're looking forward to getting away from it all on holiday next week. 5. I'm sorry, but I don't get your point. 6. Will we get our money's worth if we book the larger hotel room? 7. Paul used to get along with the twins really well. 8. I don't believe Marge will get cold feet about speaking at the conference tomorrow. 9. Is the building noise outside getting on your nerves too? 10. It feels like we're getting nowhere with this discussion. 11. We just could not get into the last season of Mad Men. 12. Did Kerri really just tell her father to get lost? 13. *You* are going to be a *model*? Get away! 14. If you won't get your act together, then you leave me no choice but to give you the sack. 15. Did your auntie's comments get to you

Answers to Worksheets and Notes for Use

last night? Don't be upset. 16. If I tried wakeboarding, I'm sure I would get a feel for it. 17. Yes – you need to get a life! There! I said it! 18. Will you get a move on and choose something from the menu, please? 19. Olivia got a kick out of seeing her brother upset. 20. If we don't leave now, we won't get a head start on the traffic.

86   Answers will vary.

87   1. make. 2. do. 3. do. 4. make. 5. do. 6. do. 7. make. 8. make. 9. do. 10. make. 11. do. 12. make. 13. make. 14. do. 15. make. 16. do. 17. do. 18. make. 19. do. 20. do. 21. do. 22. make. 23. make. 24. make. 25. do. 26. do. 27. make. 28. do. 29. make. 30. do. 31. make. 32. make. 33. do. 34. make. 35. make. 36. do. 37. make. 38. make. 39. make. 40. make.

88   1. do. 2. make. 3. do. 4. make. 5. make. 6. do. 7. make. 8. make. 9. do. 10. do. 11. make. 12. make. 13. do. 14. make. 15. make. 16. make. 17. do. 18. make. 19. make. 20. make. 21. do. 22. make. 23. make. 24. do. 25. make. 26. make. 27. do. 28. do. 29. make. 30. make. 31. do. 32. make. 33. do. 34. make. 35. do. 36. make. 37. do. 38. do. 39. do. 40. make.

89   1. were doing. 2. to make. 3. are making. 4. was doing. 5. has done. 6. to make. 7. have been doing. 8. 's been making. 9. do. 10. had made. 11. do, make. 12. had done, have made. 13. will have done. 14. made, making. 15. will do. 16. will make. 17. make, do, make. 18. made, make. 19. did. 20. to make, will do.

91   1. Keep the **kids'** brains active during the holidays with our great summer school! (A) 2. Are you fed up with reading about **others'** good fortune? (A) 3. Newcastle, **it is clear,** is a city of great contrasts. (E) 4. I had told the papers that I didn't **[extra word: had]** want to talk to them, but they still followed me into the hotel. (F) 5. We can go by car, or it's about twenty **minutes'** walk from here. (A) 6. We were glad that the councillors were able to stay **[extra word: did]** for the whole afternoon. (F) 7. When you see our prices you won't **believe** your eyes! (G) 8. The children's play train is now boarding. Get on **board!** (G) 9. An umbrella that stays up when it gets windy – what **a** great idea! (B) 10. Are you going out on New **Year's** Eve? (A) 11. Thinking of learning to hang-glide? You'll soon **get** the hang of it! (G) 12. The station is only about thirty-five **minutes'** drive away. (A) 13. Adult **tickets** – £4.60. (G) 14. We are aiming to improve **individuals'** skills with our new computer courses. (A) 15. Children will be able **[missing word: to]** compete in four different age categories. (F) 16. Make Someone **Happy** Today – Smile! (C) 17. If things aren't going well, why not **take a** new course of action? (D) 18. We're all really looking forward to the wedding on October 8th! (D) 19. Our products offer solutions to a range of **everyday** IT and wireless communication needs. (G) 20. We are working hard to improve our store so that it will be, **without question,** the best hardware store in the city. (E)

92   1. **It's** worth asking about our amazing offers! (A) 2. This ticket is valid for any **Friday** or Saturday in December. (C) 3. A few months **ago** I was earning £650 per month for 30 hours per week. Since then my salary has doubled. (G) 4. Have you read Bridget **Jones's** Diary? (A) 5. Jennifer Jameson, **our accountant,** is due to retire at the end of next month. (E) 6. Do you know how many **European** countries have signed up to the single currency?(G) 7. He's a spy, a con-man, a lover, and a **thief.** Now he's back for a new adventure. (G) 8. The new Ford Focus is in a different class from **[fewer words, e.g. its predecessors].** (D) 9. You are welcome to join us in church

Answers to Worksheets and Notes for Use

for **an** Easter celebration. (B) 10. The information about Richard and Tina's [**missing word or words, e.g. business**] originated from reliable sources. (F) 11. Every **Monday** night is party night at McCoy's. (C) 12. Become a teaching assistant and make a real difference to a **child's** life. (A) 13. You can find us on **St. John's** Street, near the post office. (A) 14. Children under 8 years old must be [**extra word: with**] accompanied by an adult. (F) 15. SALE! Robbie **Williams's** latest album is half-price for a limited time only. (A) 16. We will be open **all day** on Sunday. (G) 17. Our stores are now open **every day** of the week. (G) 18. You are what you **eat**, or so they say. (G) 19. Half of the managers were [**missing word, e.g. for**] the proposals and half were against. It was an even split. (F) 20. This car has got the lot – **style**, speed, and a dazzling array of extras. (C)

93   1. Packaging design is *so* important! An eye-catching design can make all the difference to the number of products sold. (D) 2. Can you book the room a few **days** before you plan to come? (A) 3. Special offer – get up to 12 **months'** half price line rental on all feature phones. (A) 4. Kojak's **Hair** Salon – open Monday to Saturday. Late opening on Wednesdays. (C) 5. So many **people** enjoy the peaceful scenery at Sandcastle Gardens. (G) 6. For more details about any of our products, please contact **Laura** on 01332 442 5900. (C) 7. If you would like to hire a tennis court please [**missing word, e.g. ask**] a member of staff. 8. **It's** sale time at Harrington's Department Store! (A) 9. Computer printer cartridges will be on offer throughout the month [**extra word: on**] of June. (F) 10. Do your children spend every weekend **poring** over their school books? (G) 11. All of the people on the committee will have to [**extra words: come, of**] attend the annual meeting. (F) 12. I haven't seen my family since last **Christmas** Eve. (A) 13. I need at least two **days'** notice if you want to come with me to Birmingham. (A) 14. The office of Allen's Solicitors has recently been refurbished, so there shouldn't be **any more** building work in the foreseeable future. (G) 15. We would like to welcome you to our latest **catalogue**. (G) 16. What are your New **Year's** resolutions? (A) 17. The plane left on schedule but, **unbelievably,** we were still late arriving in Singapore. (E) 18. We are now booking for **New Year's Eve**. (C) 19. Our company is offering **a** new opportunity for school leavers. (B) 20. I'm really looking forward to getting a new karaoke machine **next month**. (D)

94   1. We offer the best deal in town on tyres and **exhausts**. (G) 2. An impolite tortoise can make its owner's life a misery. (A) 3. It's only £5.99 per person for three games of bowling. (A) 4. The deputy manager, **who is on holiday,** will deal with your enquiry very soon. (E) 5. Coming soon – "A **Midsummer Night's** Dream". (A) 6. The 15.15 train service to Leicester has been **cancelled**. (G) 7. Come to the Old King's Head and enjoy a 3-course meal for only £8.99. At the Old **King's** Head we pride ourselves on the quality of our service. (A) 8. Paulo's – **the** no.1 Italian restaurant in the Greater London area. (B) 9. John and Jenny **Lewis's** family-run hotel is an enchanting place to stay. (A) 10. This **year's** school concert will have something for everyone. (A) 11. See you in an **hour's** time. (A) 12. We will be closed for business from Friday 14ᵗʰ May until Tuesday 18ᵗʰ May. **If you have any enquiries, please call us on...** (D) 13. The date when a library book is due back is stamped on **the** first page of the book. (B) 14. For the best deals in town – get down to **Mark's Bargain Basement**. (C) 15. Come and visit **Mrs. Johnson's** Tea Rooms (turn left after the bridge). (A) 16. If you would like to apply for the **vacancy**, please email your CV to... (G) 17. Have you tried Harvey's Bistro yet? (D) 18. If you wait, the receptionist will arrange **an** appointment for you. (B) 19. "Nico's Business Tips" is a new programme

Answers to Worksheets and Notes for Use

especially **[extra word: just]** for would-be tycoons. (F) 20. Please make all cheques payable to **Mr.** Phil Sanders. (C)

95   Note for pages 95-98: we use polite language in formal situations and with people that we don't know well. We may also use polite language when we need to ask somebody we know for a favour. We don't need to use polite language all the time. If we did we would sound very strange! We use neutral language in everyday informal situations, with family and friends, as well as with people that we know well. We use rude language when we are angry or upset, or if we are feeling stressed. We may use it with family and friends as well as with people we don't know. It may be better to find ways of avoiding the use of rude language, because it does tend to make a bad situation worse, rather than help resolve it – although you may feel better because you have let off steam! Read the situations on the four worksheets and decide which type of language is most likely to be used – polite, neutral, or rude. Compare the different responses and discuss why they may or may not be appropriate.

Answers: Situation 1: a) Polite. Situation 2: b) Neutral. Situation 3: a) Polite. Situation 4: b) Neutral or c) Rude – depending on how you choose to handle the situation!

96   Situation 5: b) Neutral. Situation 6: a) Polite. Situation 7: b) Neutral. Situation 8: a) Polite.

97   Situation 9: b) Neutral. Situation 10: b) Neutral or c) Rude – depending on how you choose to handle the situation! Situation 11: c) Rude. Situation 12: b) Neutral.

98   Situation 13: b) Neutral or c) Rude – depending on how you choose to handle the situation! Situation 14: a) Polite. Situation 15: b) Neutral or c) Rude – depending on how you choose to handle the situation!

100   1. awfully nice. 2. bad luck. 3. non-alcoholic beer. 4. common courtesy. 5. foreign national. 6. tough love. 7. young adult. 8. student teacher. 9. perfectly normal. 10. school holiday. 11. safety hazard. 12. relative stranger. 13. open secret. 14. recent past. 15. act naturally. 16. absolutely unsure. 17. deafening silence. 18. same difference. 19. group of individuals. 20. incredibly dull. 21. intense apathy. 22. social outcast. 23. safe bet. 24. accurate estimate. 25. modern history. 26. all alone. 27. eloquent silence. 28. completely destroyed. 29. numbing sensation. 30. unbiased opinion.